The Handbook of Riding Essentials

# The Handbook of

HarperCollins*Publishers*

# François Lemaire de Ruffieu

with illustrations by the author

# Riding Essentials

*Designer: Charlotte Staub*

Library of Congress Cataloging-in-Publication Data

Lemaire de Ruffieu, François.
    The handbook of riding essentials.

    Includes index.
    1. Riding aids. 2. Horsemanship. I. Title.
SF309.L44   1986        798.2'3        85-45208
ISBN 0-06-015517-5

    95 RRD 10 9 8

This book is dedicated to the memory of my dear friend David Winton, who had a very promising future as a trainer and show rider under the colors of Barrington Farms in Los Angeles.

This book is also dedicated to all my dear students and friends who have frequently asked me to condense what I teach into print.

I particularly wish to express my appreciation to Beverly Pellegrini, who, realizing how clumsy I am with the typewriter, so graciously offered her assistance.

# Contents

# Introduction

The **aids** are the means by which the rider communicates his or her will to the horse. **Artificial aids,** such as whips, spurs, longe whips, and all types of special tack, can be very effective when properly used. But the secret of equitation lies in the use of the **natural aids**— the seat, the hands, and the legs. To develop tact and authority, you need both a thorough mastery of these aids and a perfect understanding of their function.

**Tact,** in the equestrian sense, is the ability to choose, either by instinct or after quick thought, the most appropriate actions to obtain a specific response from your horse. Correct timing, intensity, and duration of the application of the aids should directly correspond to the physical and mental reactions of your horse.

Authority is acquired through knowledge and skill.

- A novice rider corrects the horse's mistake after it occurs.
- A good rider corrects the mistake when it occurs.
- An educated rider *prevents* the mistake.

Anger, a sign of frustration, results from lack of knowledge.

A rider improves his or her skill through feeling. When you have to lean over to see your horse's motion under you, you unconsciously lessen the development of your sense of feel. *In equitation, to feel is to understand.*

Often, during the clinics I give in the United States and in Europe, I meet riders who know so little about, or just forget how, why, and when, the natural aids are used. In my opinion, it is mandatory to know, *by heart,* what must be done to obtain a specific movement from your horse.

An educated rider will realize that using the natural aids properly for flat work will improve jumping performance as well and give his or her horse a chance to reach the High School Dressage.

This book does not claim to explain a new method of horseback riding, but only to simplify what some of the best European masters have left behind. In Part I, I explain what the natural aids are and describe how they are applied. Part II explains how to coordinate these aids for the five different rein actions, at the various gaits, and for transitions. Finally, in Part III, I show how to apply the principles developed in the book to advanced exercises for the horse. I also, from time to time, propose a training procedure. There are several other approaches to learning or teaching each movement, but in this book I will only describe the ones that have worked best for me and my students.

François

# Part One

# BASIC PRINCIPLES

# The Natural Aids and How They Are Used

The principal natural aids are the seat, the hands, and the legs.

## The Seat

The term **seat** is used to refer to the distribution of the rider's weight on the buttocks and ischia (seat bones). The seat has a tremendous influence on the horse's balance:

- Leaning forward causes the horse to increase speed.
- Leaning backwards causes the horse to slow down.
- Increasing your weight on the seat bone and stirrup iron on one side causes the horse to bear in that direction.

Your weight must always be oriented in the direction of your horse's motion. Proper use of the seat sets the rhythm of the pace and gives the impression of smoothness at the different gaits.

The term seat is also used to refer to the way the rider sits in the saddle. A rider is said to have a good seat when he or she moves in total harmony with the horse. A good seat is a quality you must have to control your balance in all circumstances, regardless of your horse's reactions. It requires suppleness and relaxation of the lower back, which acts as a shock absorber.

## The Hands

The hands act, resist, and yield through the reins to regulate the horse's forward motion.

**Fig. 1**

**Fig. 2**

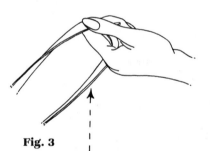

**Fig. 3**

### How do the hands act?

The hands act to slow the speed, change the gaits (downward), modify the horse's balance, and give direction.

They always act *without pulling*:

- By squeezing the fingers on the reins (see Fig. 1).
- By turning the wrists, fingernails up (like turning a doorknob) to increase the tension (see Fig. 2).
- By raising the wrists 2 to 3 inches, to further increase the tension (see Fig. 3). You can increase the tension still further by leaning the upper body backwards.

These actions are the *progressive* steps to obtain obedience. They must be of brief duration and repeated if necessary.

### How do the hands resist?

The hands resist to oppose any undesirable initiative taken by the horse. Their resistance should be equal to the horse's, but not greater:

- By insisting (i.e., squeezing the fingers on the reins without pulling) *until* the horse has submitted.

### How do the hands yield?

The hands yield to reward obedience as soon as the horse has obeyed, without losing contact with the horse's mouth:

- By lowering the wrists.
- By moving the wrists forward.
- By opening the fingers.

These actions are the *progressive* steps to reward obedience.

## The Legs

The legs act, resist, and yield to produce and maintain the horse's forward motion—to change the gait (upwards) and increase the speed. They are also used to position the horse's hindquarters and **engage** his hind legs (cause him to bring his hind legs forward and directly under his body). They create and sustain **impulsion,** which is both the horse's attentiveness and the actual will or energy that makes him respond to the rider's commands.

### How do the legs act?

The legs act together **at the girth** (actually 4 to 6 inches behind—see Fig. 4) to drive the horse forward:

- By squeezing and releasing the calves continuously.
- By squeezing and releasing the heels.
- By kicking with the heels.

The legs act individually **behind the girth** (actually about 8 to 10 inches behind—see Fig. 4) to make the horse move his hindquarters (the horse's response to this individual leg pressure is also called **leg yielding**):

- By squeezing and releasing the calves continuously.
- By squeezing and releasing the heels.
- By kicking with the heels.

at the girth    behind the girth

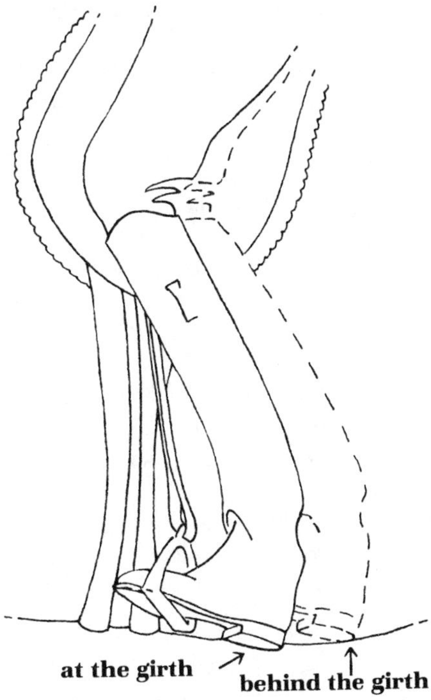

Fig. 4

These actions are the *progressive* steps to obtain obedience.

### How do the legs resist?

The legs resist to prevent or oppose a lateral displacement of the horse's haunches:

- By maintaining pressure with the calves or the heels.
- By kicking if necessary.

### How do the legs yield?

The legs yield to reward obedience:

- By ceasing to act or resist.    • By lightening their pressure.

Your legs should always stay in light contact with the horse's barrel, so that they are ready to act without startling the horse by a sudden movement. When you begin training your horse, your legs will have to act strongly to obtain obedience; as your horse progresses, he will become more sensitive to the aids and your leg action can be more gentle.

---

*All my life I have heard some instructors scream, "Squeeze your knees!" and others, "Squeeze your calves!" Who is right?*

*Let us take the example of two fingers squeezing an empty soda can held horizontally. When you squeeze the can with your thumb and index finger above the center, it slides from your grasp. When you squeeze below the center, you crush the can without dropping it.*

*On a horse, the principle is the same. If you squeeze with your upper legs and knees, the pressure is applied above the widest part of the horse's barrel. You could be thrown if your horse bucks or stops suddenly. If, however, you squeeze below the midpoint of your horse's barrel, with your calves, you will be glued to the saddle and able to follow your horse's reactions in all circumstances.*

*If you are at a halt, squeezing with your thighs and knees will produce no reaction whatsoever, but squeezing with your calves and heels will cause your horse to move forward.*

---

## The Voice, the Eyes, and the Mind

The rider's voice, eyes, and mind, also considered natural aids, are rarely mentioned, but are very important.

## The Natural Aids and How They Are Used

### The voice

The rider's voice is indispensable for teaching a young horse. Your tone of voice creates confidence and respect:

- A quiet voice calms the horse.
- A loud voice upsets the horse.

Words remind the horse what to do and it is most important not to confuse him. You must have a specific word that you use all the time for each command. I have often heard riders shouting "whoa!" at different commands. Would you say "trot" when you want to canter?

As the training of your horse progresses, you *must* replace your voice commands with leg and hand actions. If your horse is green, voice commands are acceptable, but in most other cases they are a sign of the rider's insecurity and lack of authority.

### The eyes

The rider's eyes, attentive to the direction, initiate the use of the appropriate aids. When you ride a bicycle, for example, you only have to look in the direction you are heading, and instinctively your legs and hands will do whatever is necessary to make a turn. Similarly, on a horse, if you have mastered the use of your aids, your response will be automatic. *Always look in the direction you want your horse to go.*

### The mind

Is the mind the most important natural aid?

Without elaborating on this complex subject, I will simply mention some very important points. Every rider should think about them. They are the keys to success.

- You should train yourself to react promptly. The best way to develop good reflexes is to understand and then to learn, by heart, how and why the natural aids act, resist, and yield. Taking notes or reviewing information in your head before going to sleep is an excellent way to assimilate knowledge.
- You must remember that horses are also beings. They work hard. They get tired. They have likes and dislikes. They are brave or shy. They need love without being too spoiled.

- You need to set goals: small goals at first, and then, eventually, more ambitious ones.
- To solve a major problem, you should break it down into little problems and deal with them one at a time.

## The Artificial Aids

When needed, artificial aids come in handy to reinforce the natural aids. They include special tack, such as the Chambon, Gogue, draw reins, Colbert reins, side reins, rigid reins, martingales of any type, and anything else a rider may need to impose his or her will on the horse. These artificial aids are very helpful in the hands of an expert, but giving them to a novice rider can be like putting a razor blade in a monkey's hand.

The whip, the spurs, and the longe whip can be used without harm by most riders.

### The whip (crop, bat)
- Used on the shoulder, it stimulates a lazy horse.
- Used on the flanks, it extends the above action.
- Used on the rump, it punishes disobedience.

The whip is a very important aid in training, when it is used to teach and reinforce the actions of the legs. It must be used with authority, never anger.

### The spurs
The spurs, symbol of the true rider, reinforce the actions of the legs. They should come in contact with the horse's barrel only when the rider desires it. Spurs are not a tool for the novice with loose legs.

### The longe whip
The longe whip is used for ground work, especially with the longe line.

- Used on the hindquarters, it creates and stimulates the forward motion.

- Used on the hind legs, it improves the engagement.
- Used in front of the horse, it slows or stops him.

The longe whip must be used with discretion and authority, never anger. The horse has to learn to respect it without being afraid of it. When you are using the longe whip, it is better to make the lash whistle than to crack it—leave that to the lion tamers.

## Accord of the Aids

The accord of the aids is the harmonious coordination of all the natural aids. Together, the seat, hands, and legs act, resist, and yield to create, regulate, and facilitate the correct execution of the different movements demanded by the rider. You have to learn to coordinate your hands, coordinate your legs, and coordinate your hands with your legs.

- Your seat sets the rhythm of the gaits.
- Your hands control the horse's forehand, i.e. your left hand controls the horse's left foreleg, and your right hand controls the horse's right foreleg.
- Your legs control the horse's hindquarters, i.e. your left leg controls the horse's left hind leg, and your right leg controls the horse's right hind leg.
- Your legs create the impulsion and your hands regulate it.

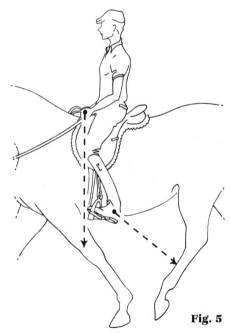

Fig. 5

There should be constant rapport between the hands and legs. They must never work against each other. Lengthening and shortening the gaits (see pages 66–68) is an excellent exercise that will improve coordination of the hands and legs. The lateral movements (see pages 73–96) help you coordinate the aids in lateral or diagonal pairs.

# The Rider's Position

**I**n order to coordinate the natural aids properly, you must maintain the correct position in and out of the saddle.

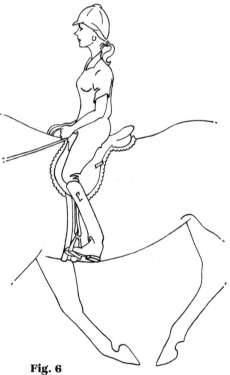

**Fig. 6**

### In the Saddle

- You sit comfortably on your seat bones (ischia) in the deepest part of the saddle.
- Your lower back is supple, supported without stiffness, and ready to move in all directions.
- Your upper body is comfortable, straight, and free.
- Your shoulders, equally open, are totally relaxed.
- Your head is held high and straight.
- Your eyes are attentive to the direction.
- Your arms, elbows bent, drop naturally by your sides.
- Your wrists are held in line with your forearms.
- Your hands, on the same line as your forearms, are held 4 to 5 inches apart.

- Your thumbs and index fingers hold the reins firmly, the thumb nails facing up.
- Your thighs, dropped naturally, are in light contact with the saddle.
- Your knees are in light contact with the saddle.
- Your lower legs (calves) are in contact with the horse's barrel. The stirrup leather should be perpendicular to the ground.
- Your ankles are relaxed and springy.
- Your feet are at the girth (actually 4 to 6 inches behind):

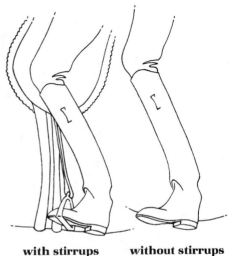

*With stirrups:* Lightly hold each stirrup base by the balls of your feet, with more weight on the inside of the stirrup iron. Your heels are lower than your toes. Each stirrup iron is almost perpendicular to the horse's body, the outside branch pointing slightly forward. (See Fig. 7.)

*Without stirrups:* Let your feet drop naturally by their own weight; the toes may be higher than the heels. (See Fig. 7.)

This position does not require special muscular contractions and can be held for a long time without fatigue.

**with stirrups**    **without stirrups**

**Fig. 7**

## Out of the Saddle

This position is used for jumping or speed and is called the hunt seat, forward seat, 2-point, suspension seat, or half seat. The only differences between the sitting and the standing positions are in the seat, the upper body, and the feet.

- Your seat is slightly out of the saddle, but directly above your feet.
- Your upper body is comfortable, tilted slightly forward. The faster the speed is, the more tilted your upper body will be.
- Your ankles are flexed, but are also relaxed and springy.
- Your feet, at the girth, have more weight in the heels, and stay directly under the seat.

## Checking Your Position

*Have you ever seen a baby trying to walk for the first time? The only way he or she can manage is by leaning on furniture or other objects. As soon as babies learn to bring their feet directly under them, they no longer need to use their hands for support. If you have to rely on the reins, the stirrups, or the pommel of the saddle to stay on your horse, you have not yet mastered your balance. Like a baby, you have to keep your balance by placing your legs under your seat.*

Mounted, you can determine the proper position of your feet by glancing down at your knees. If you can see your toes, your lower legs are too far forward.

You can check the length of the stirrups either from the ground or mounted.

*From the ground:* Stand at the horse's left side and put the fingertips of your right hand on the stirrup safety bar. With your left hand, pull the stirrup leather, including the iron, to the armpit of your outstretched right arm (so that the leather is the length of your arm), and secure the buckle. (If you are a beginner, riding with shorter stirrups, apply the same method with your right hand in a fist.)

*Mounted:* Let the stirrup hang free of your foot. The sole of your boot should be level with the stirrup base. (For a beginner, the sole of the boot should be 2 to 3 inches below the stirrup base.)

At the walk, trot, and canter, the withers is the only part of the horse's body that remains relatively still. To be comfortable, you should sit in the deepest part of the saddle, which is over the back end of the withers. Sitting on your seat bones, you should have the feeling that the horse is in front of you, easy to guide. If you sat on your crotch, you would have the feeling that the horse is behind you. A bad seat can cause problems: Have you ever noticed that some riders, regardless of the horse they ride, always encounter the same difficulties, such as loss of control, rearing, bucking, and so on?

## Holding the Reins

Your hands should stay at a fixed distance from the horse's mouth and the reins must be adjusted, forming a straight line from the bit to your hands. If the reins are slack or flap about, your commands may not reach your horse's mouth, or they may confuse him. Worse, your hand actions may reach your horse's mouth in the form of brutal or awkward jerks.

There are several ways to hold the reins:

### Held separately, one in each hand

- The reins come into your hands either under the pinky finger or above it, whichever is most comfortable.
- The reins come out of your hands between the thumb and index finger (see Fig. 8).
- The bight of the reins (the free end with the buckle) hangs to the right on the horse's shoulder.

**Fig. 8**

### Held in the left hand

- The reins come into your left hand on each side of the pinky finger, the left rein under it, the right rein above it.
- The reins come out of your hand together, held between the thumb and index finger (see Fig. 9).
- The bight of the reins hangs to the right on the horse's shoulder.

**Fig. 9**

### Held in the right hand

- The reins come into your right hand on each side of the index finger, the left rein between the thumb and index finger and the right rein between the index and the third finger.
- The reins come out of the hand together, under the palm.
- The bight of the reins hangs to the right on the horse's shoulder (see Fig. 10).

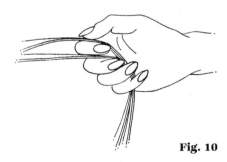

**Fig. 10**

The reins should never get in your way. It's a good idea to practice switching them from one hand to the other. This is an excellent training exercise that does not interfere with the pace and teaches you to consider your horse's mouth. Once you have decided what is most comfortable for you, you can avoid unnecessary confusion by always holding the reins the same way.

# Exercises for the Rider

**T**here are 3 criteria for applying the aids properly:

1. Suppleness: Flexibility of the joints.
2. Fixity: Absence of unnecessary movement.
3. Comfort: Freedom of the body and mind.

To improve and develop suppleness, fixity, and comfort in the saddle, stretch the muscles of your legs and your upper body, using the exercises below. They should be done without stirrups, first at a halt and then at the walk, trot, and canter. If you have someone to help you, it is preferable to do the exercises on the longe line first. The leg and upper body exercises should be preceded and followed by a correction of the seat exercise and short periods of trotting with and without stirrups (see below).

## Correcting Your Seat

If you are having trouble sitting forward in the saddle, you can correct your seat with the following exercise:

- Hold on to the pommel with one or both hands (see Fig. 11a).
- Lean the upper body back slightly (see Fig. 11b).
- Raise both knees, being careful not to kick your horse, and at the same time, pull firmly on the pommel to slide your seat as far forward as possible (see Fig. 11c).

- Energetically kick your heels down to stretch your muscles and bring your legs back to the correct position (see Fig. 11d).

Practice will make this seat position very comfortable even though human beings were not born to sit this way.

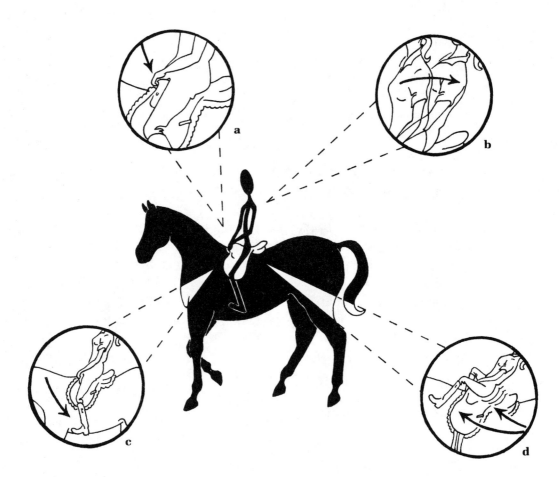

**Fig. 11**

## Leg Exercises

1. Alternately and then simultaneously raise each leg, bending the knee, and kick down firmly, heel first (see Fig. 12a).
2. Alternately and then simultaneously raise each leg, bending the knee, and kick back firmly, heel first (see Fig. 12b).
3. Stretch your left hand forward, level with your shoulder, palm facing down. With your left foot, kick your left hand. Do the same with the right foot and right hand. (See Fig. 13.) This can also be done with both legs and both hands at the same time.
4. At the walk and trot, hold on to the pommel and keep your knees up for a few seconds. (See Fig. 14.)
5. Rotate your feet clockwise and counterclockwise. (See Fig. 15.)
6. Drop and pick up your stirrups, first on each side separately, then on both sides simultaneously.

**Fig. 12**

**Fig. 13**

**Fig. 14**

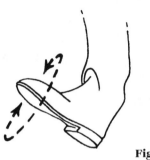

**Fig. 15**

Fig. 16

## Upper Body Exercises

1. Slowly lean back until your shoulders touch your horse's croup. Your legs remain still. Bring your upper body up by tightening your heels. (See Fig. 16.)
2. With your arms stretched out in front of you, draw large circles around your shoulders, clockwise and counterclockwise, first with each arm separately and then with both together. While your arms are rotating, follow your hands' motion with your eyes. (See Fig. 17.)
3. With arms stretched out to the sides at shoulder level, palms up, twist your upper body to the right and left. At each twist, look behind you. (See Fig. 18.)

You can develop the independence of your legs and hands by combining some of the leg and upper body exercises.

Fig. 17

Fig. 18

## Trotting Without Stirrups

The sitting trot without stirrups is an excellent exercise for improving and securing the seat while giving independence to the upper body. It should be done initially by holding the pommel with one hand. As your lower legs get tighter around the horse's barrel, you can reduce the number of fingers on the pommel. With practice you will no longer need to hold on to keep your balance.

The posting trot without stirrups is wonderful for strengthening the contact of your calves with the horse's barrel and for improving your balance. Pretending you are using stirrups, raise both your knees and your toes, squeeze your lower legs and begin posting. Do not cheat yourself by squeezing your knees.

## Breathing

You *must* learn to breathe properly. Breathing too fast can exhaust you or give you a stitch in the side. At the trot and canter, you should inhale slowly during two or three strides and exhale in the same way. At the walk, you can breathe normally, since the pace is slower.

# Part Two

# COORDINATING THE
# NATURAL AIDS

# The Natural Aids
# for Rein Actions

There are five different rein actions:

( I ) **Direct Rein**
- For turns.
- For changes of direction.
- For the half-pass.

( II ) **Direct Rein of Opposition**
- For sharp changes of direction.
- For the canter depart (outside lateral aids).

( III ) **Indirect Rein**
- For maintaining or correcting direction and balance.
- For the haunches-in.
- For the half-turn on the haunches.

( IV ) **Indirect Rein of Opposition in Front of the Withers**
- For the canter depart (diagonal aids and inside lateral aids).
- For the half-turn on the forehand.

( V ) **Indirect Rein of Opposition Behind the Withers**
- For the shoulder-in.

These rein actions require careful coordination of **active** and **passive** aids.

A hand that affects the equilibrium or the impulsion of the horse is called an **active hand.** A **passive hand** preserves the contact with the horse's mouth, but does not oppose either the horse's impulsion or the active hand (there is accord between the hands).

A leg that creates the impulsion or the engagement, or modifies the position of the hindquarters is called an **active leg.** A **passive leg** maintains the impulsion by applying lighter contact than the active leg, without opposing it.

When the active aids are placed on the same side of the horse (i.e., right hand, right leg), they are called **lateral aids.** When the active aids are placed on opposite sides of the horse (i.e., right hand, left leg), they are called **diagonal aids.** *The secret of good riding is the ability to combine all the lateral and diagonal aids properly.*

*Note: For easy identification, the five rein actions will be labeled throughout the book with circled roman numerals. All instructions are given for the right rein. They should be reversed for the left rein. The illustrations were designed for quick reference: the black foot indicates that that leg is performing functions other than simply maintaining the impulsion; the black dot on the saddle stands for the seat bone receiving more weight.*

## Ⓘ Direct Rein (Leading or Opening Rein)

### Rider's aids

Right hand: Active, rotates at the wrist, fingernails facing up. The movement of the hand is forward and to the right; the elbow remains in the hip area.

Left hand: Passive, goes forward and down to yield, to allow, and then to regulate the action of the right hand.

Right leg: Active at the girth, slightly more forward than normal.

Left leg: Active at the girth to maintain the impulsion.

Seat: More weight on the right seat bone.

### Horse's response

Nose: Moves to the right.

Head: Moves to the right.

Neck: Bends to the right.

Shoulders: The right carries more weight than the left.

Haunches: No action.

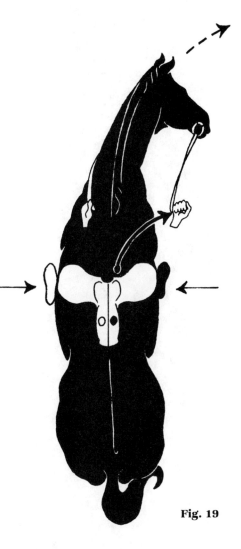

**Fig. 19**

*Result:* The horse turns to the right with his haunches following the same path as his forehand.

## ⓘⓘ **Direct Rein of Opposition**

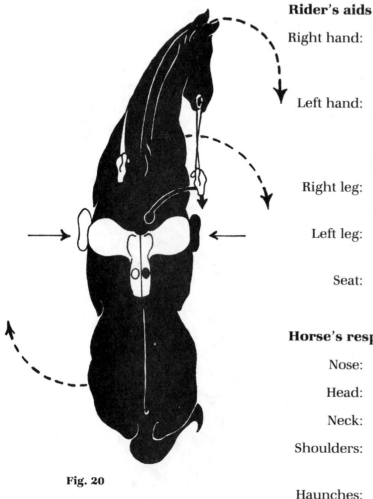

**Rider's aids**

Right hand: Active, moves a few inches to the right and applies tension to the rear.

Left hand: Passive, goes forward and down to yield, to allow, and then to regulate the action of the right hand.

Right leg: Active at the girth, slightly stronger than the left.

Left leg: Active at the girth to maintain the impulsion.

Seat: More weight on the right seat bone.

**Horse's response**

Nose: Moves to the right and back.

Head: Moves to the right and back.

Neck: Bends sharply to the right.

Shoulders: The right carries more weight than the left.

Haunches: Swing to the left.

**Fig. 20**

*Result:* The horse turns very sharply to the right with his haunches making a wider turn than his forehand.

## III Indirect Rein (Western, Supporting, Bearing, and Neck Rein)

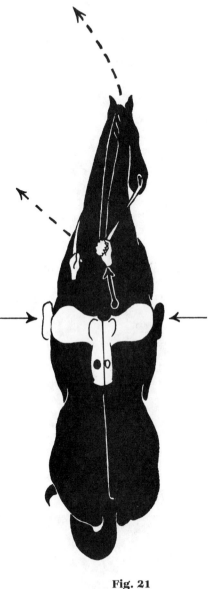

### Rider's aids

Right hand:  Active, rotates at the wrist, fingernails facing up for more strength; moves forward and slightly toward the left on the neck.

Left hand:  Passive, goes forward and down to yield, to allow, and then to regulate the action of the right hand.

Right leg:  Active at the girth, slightly stronger than the left, to forbid the haunches from drifting to the right.

Left leg:  Active at the girth to maintain the impulsion.

Seat:  More weight on the left seat bone.

### Horse's response

Nose:  Moves slightly to the right.

Head:  The top pivots to the left.

Neck:  Curves very slightly to the right.

Shoulders:  The left carries more weight than the right.

Haunches:  May swing to the right.

**Fig. 21**

*Result:*  The horse bears to the left with his haunches following the same path as his forehand.

## $\text{IV}$ Indirect Rein of Opposition in Front of the Withers

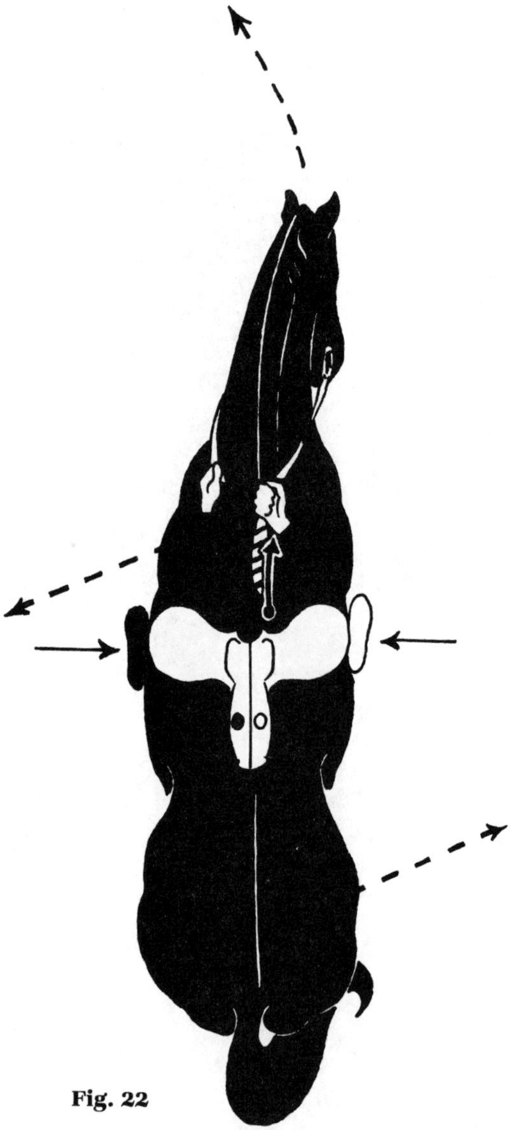

**Rider's aids**

Right hand: Active, rotates at the wrist, fingernails facing up; acts slightly to the left in front of the withers.

Left hand: Passive, goes forward and down to yield, to allow, and then to regulate the action of the right hand.

Right leg: Active at the girth to maintain the impulsion.

Left leg: Active, slightly behind the girth, stronger than the right, to encourage the haunches to go right when needed.

Seat: More weight on the left seat bone.

**Horse's response**

Nose: Moves to the right and back.

Head: Moves to the right and back.

Neck: Curves to the right.

Shoulders: The left carries more weight than the right.

Haunches: Swing to the right.

**Fig. 22**

*Result:* The horse pivots around his gravity center, his forehand going left, his haunches going right.

## (V)  Indirect Rein of Opposition Behind the Withers (Intermediate Rein)

### Rider's aids

Right hand: Active, rotates at the wrist, fingernails facing up; acts slightly to the left behind the withers.

Left hand: Passive, goes forward and down to yield, to allow, and then to regulate the action of the right hand.

Right leg: Active behind the girth to push the haunches to the left.

Left leg: Active at the girth to maintain the impulsion.

Seat: More weight on the left seat bone.

### Horse's response

Nose: Moves to the right and back.

Head: Moves to the right and back.

Neck: Curves to the right.

Shoulders: The left carries more weight than the right.

Haunches: Drift to the left; the left carries more weight than the right.

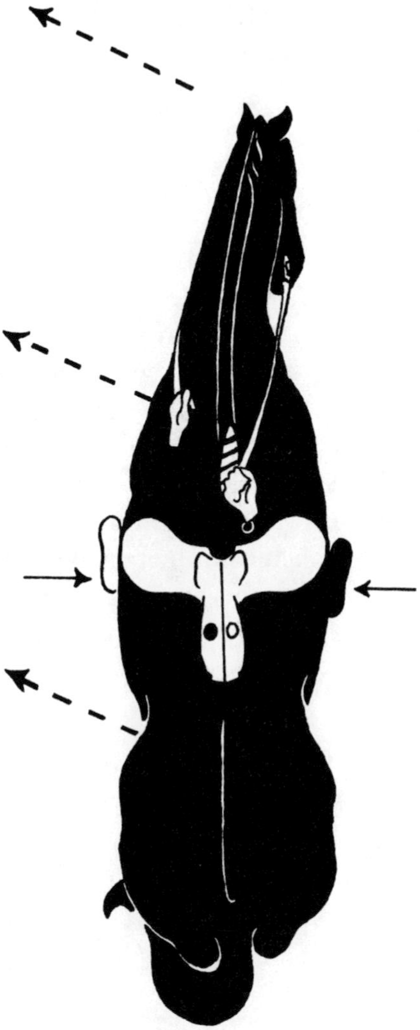

**Fig. 23**

*Result:*   The horse bears obliquely to the left; his shoulders and haunches travel on parallel tracks.

# The Natural Aids for Putting the Horse on the Bit

**A**t liberty, the horse has a natural balance that allows him to move with grace in all directions at any speed. The weight of a rider on a horse's back causes clumsiness, muscle contractions, resistance, and sometimes even rebelliousness. To minimize these problems and to ride properly, you must have your horse **on the bit.**

A horse is said to be on the bit when he is attentive to the rider's aids and has proper head carriage. His head should be held within a 45 degree angle in front of an imaginary vertical line running from his poll to his jaw (see Fig. 24).

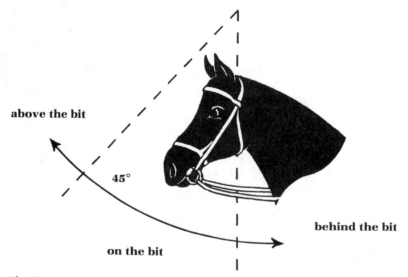

above the bit

45°

on the bit

behind the bit

**Fig. 24**

If the angle of the horse's head is greater than 45 degrees, he is said to be **above the bit** (he fights contact). If the horse flexes his neck and pulls his head in toward his chest so that his nose is behind the vertical line, he is said to be **behind the bit** (he avoids contact). If your horse is properly on the bit, you can obtain changes in balance and variations of gait or speed—in short, obedience to your slightest demand.

The expression "on the bit" implies contact. In this case, contact is the gentle relation between the horse's mouth and the rider's hands and has three different degrees:

1. Light: For flat work.
2. Soft: Slightly more marked; for jumping.
3. Firm: Suitable for a faster pace (gallop and races).

*Do not confuse putting your horse on the bit with pulling on the reins. If the contact is very light, make sure that your horse is not behind the bit.*

## How Does the Rider Put the Horse on the Bit?

Seat:   Weight is equally distributed between the 2 seat bones.

Legs:   Active at the girth to create and maintain impulsion.

Hands:   In light contact with the horse's mouth after overcoming any kind of resistance.

The horse can show two kinds of resistance: resistance of weight and resistance of force.

### Overcoming resistance of weight

Resistance of weight is caused by bad balance due to a weak back, which makes the horse lean on the bit. To correct this, execute a series of **half-halts,** using one or both hands:

• Rotate your wrists, fingernails facing up (see Fig. 2, page 14).
• Quickly and firmly raise your hands 2 to 3 inches (see Fig. 3, page 14).

The purpose of the half-halt is to lift the horse's neck slightly and shift his weight from his forehand to his haunches. It has no effect on either the gait or the pace.

Resistance of weight can also be eliminated by an exercise called the **neck extension.** This exercise makes the horse lower his head and neck, correcting his balance by engaging his hind legs further and making him round his spinal column.

- Raise your hands a few inches to a foot above the saddle.
- Apply firm and equal tension on both reins.
- Create impulsion by applying pressure at the girth.
- When your horse starts pulling down on the bit, yield with your hands to allow his head and neck to descend and stretch forward (see Fig. 25).

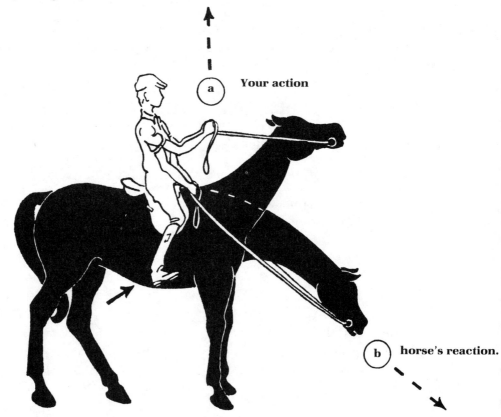

**Fig. 25**

## Putting the Horse on the Bit

*Horses seem to have an inborn aversion to what I call **fixed points.** Imagine a horse tethered to cross-ties. If he is suddenly frightened, he will bound forwards and backwards in an attempt to bolt, but will be restrained by the tension of the cross-ties on his halter. The halter becomes a fixed point. If the horse is not immediately calmed, he will fight against the halter to free himself. When you ride and constantly pull firmly on the bit, you create a fixed point in the horse's mouth. The horse's reaction will also be to pull, but against you, i.e., forward. If the tension on his mouth comes from below the bit, the horse will pull upwards. If the tension comes from above the bit, the horse's first reaction will also be to pull upwards, to avoid the tension, but if you raise your hands and keep them above the bit, the horse will very soon pull down. That's how the neck extension works.*

Once your horse understands the neck extension exercise, you can make him execute it at the walk, trot, and canter by "combing" the reins (sliding your fingers back along the reins) every time he brings his head up. As a result, your horse should travel with his head and neck as low as possible, as if he were eating grain off the ground (see Fig. 26).

**Fig. 26**

When you first teach your horse the neck extension, you may encounter two temporary problems: an increase of speed and stumbling. The increase of speed lessens as engagement improves. Stumbling forces the horse to be more careful to prevent a fall. After a few days of practice, when balance and proper engagement are attained, these two problems should disappear.

To strengthen your horse's back, you should ride him with his nose as low as possible for several weeks or even a few months. (Muscles take time to stretch and develop.) When the goals of the neck extension have been reached, it is time for you to bring your horse's head and neck back to a normal position. To do this, apply a series of tactful, but firm, half-halts (with strong legs) over a period of a few days, until your horse has re-elevated his head and neck.

### Overcoming resistance of force

Resistance of force is a contraction of the horse's neck and jaws. This can be corrected by vibrations on the bit (created by gentle, rapid shaking of the pinky finger on an adjusted rein), which incite the horse to chew, or by flexions.

A **lateral flexion** is a slight side-to-side rotation of the horse's head at the poll around the first 2 cervical vertebrae (known as Atlas and Axis) followed by a yielding of the jaws.

*Note: The instructions below are for a lateral flexion to the right. They should be reversed for a lateral flexion to the left.*

1. Right hand: Active, rotates at the wrist, fingernails up, to bring the horse's head slightly to the right.

   Left hand: Passive, goes forward and down to yield, to allow, and then to regulate the action of the right hand.

   Both legs: Active at the girth to create and maintain the impulsion.

2. Both hands: Apply slight resistance on the reins.

   Both legs: Active at the girth to create and maintain the impulsion.

3. Left hand: Quickly opens and closes the fingers on the reins to cause vibrations on the bit.

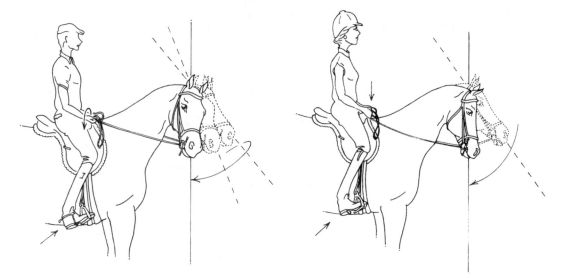

**Fig. 27** Lateral flexion.          **Fig. 28** Direct flexion.

These three stages are the *progressive* steps to obtain a lateral flexion.

At the slightest sign of a flexion, you must reward your horse by yielding with both hands. You should repeat this exercise until your horse understands it. Ask for a lateral flexion first at the halt, then at the walk, trot, and canter.

A **direct flexion** is a longitudinal rotation of the horse's head at the poll followed by a yielding of the jaws. The horse's neck remains straight and elevated.

1. Obtain several lateral flexions to the right and left sides.
2. Straighten your horse's head and then elevate his neck by executing a succession of tactful half-halts.
3. Both hands:  Apply slight tension and vibrations on the reins.

   Both legs:  Active at the girth to create and maintain the impulsion.

These three stages are the *progressive* steps to obtain a direct flexion.

At the slightest signs of a flexion, you must reward your horse by yielding with both hands. You should repeat this exercise until your horse understands it. Ask for a direct flexion first at the halt, then at the walk, trot, and canter.

---

*Dressage people often use the term* ramener *(a French word meaning to bring back) to refer to the position of the horse's head and neck as a result of a direct flexion. In this position, the horse's head is elevated and his face is held vertically. A horse is said to be* **collected** *when his head is* ramené *and his hindquarters are engaged. Collected, he is physically ready to respond to the rider's slightest demands. In high level dressage, collection is sometimes called* rassembler *(French for gather together).*

---

# The Natural Aids at the Different Gaits

**A**t the walk, trot, canter, and gallop, the horse moves his legs one or two at a time. For practical reasons, riders divide the horse's legs into pairs (bipeds):

| | |
|---:|:---|
| Front pair: | Left foreleg and right foreleg. |
| Back pair: | Left hind leg and right hind leg. |
| Right lateral pair: | Right foreleg and right hind leg. |
| Left lateral pair: | Left foreleg and left hind leg. |
| Right diagonal pair: | Right foreleg and left hind leg. |
| Left diagonal pair: | Left foreleg and right hind leg. |

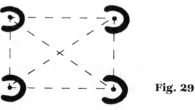

Fig. 29

A **stride** is the distance a horse can cover with all 4 legs (about 12 feet). The number of beats per stride is different for each gait.

## The Walk

At the walk, a 4-phase gait, the horse makes 4 successive beats, moving one leg at a time by diagonals. The speed is about 5 miles per hour.

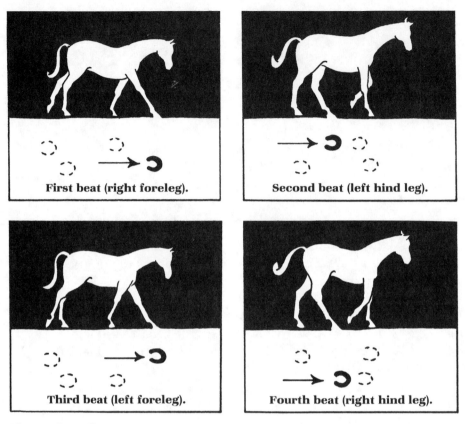

First beat (right foreleg).

Second beat (left hind leg).

Third beat (left foreleg).

Fourth beat (right hind leg).

**Fig. 30** The walk.

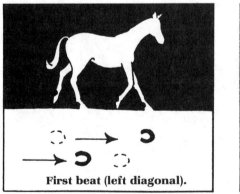
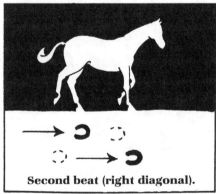

First beat (left diagonal).

Second beat (right diagonal).

**Fig. 31** The trot.

## The Trot

At the trot, a 2-phase gait, the horse makes 2 successive beats, moving 2 legs at a time by diagonals. The speed is about 9 miles per hour.

## The Canter

The canter looks like a mixture of the walk and the trot. At the canter, a 4-phase gait, the horse makes 3 successive beats followed by a suspension phase, when all 4 feet are off the ground. The horse is said to canter on either the **left** or the **right lead.** He is cantering on the left lead when his left lateral pair of legs reaches further forward

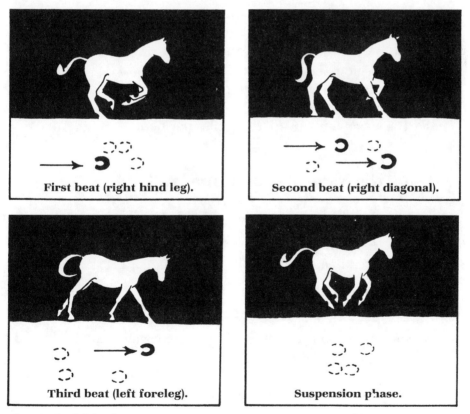

First beat (right hind leg).

Second beat (right diagonal).

Third beat (left foreleg).

Suspension phase.

**Fig. 32** The left lead canter.

49

than the right (see Fig. 32) and on the right lead when his right lateral pair of legs reaches further forward than the left. The speed is about 12 miles per hour.

The synchronization of the horse's legs at the canter may not always be easy to observe. It was only after the invention of cinematography that chronophotography helped determine in exactly what order horses move their legs when they canter. Before then, it was very difficult to describe this gait. If you look at old paintings or lithographs of horses you will find the gaits depicted interesting, but somewhat inaccurate.

## The Gallop

Although the gallop is more a racing gait than a show gait, horse show riders are sometimes asked to gallop during their classes on the flat. (Most of the time, however, these riders simply canter while in the racing position, out of the saddle.)

At the gallop, a 5-phase gait, the horse makes 4 successive beats (2 beats per diagonal starting with the hind leg) followed by a suspension phase. The speed is about 15 to 20 miles per hour.

## Using the Natural Aids at the Walk

### How does the rider use the natural aids?

Seat: Relax and swing your seat back and forth, one seat bone at a time, following the horse's motion.

Legs: Continuously increase and decrease the pressure of the inner part of the calves, one after the other.

Hands: Move your hands continuously forwards and backwards, left and right.

### Why does the rider use the natural aids?

At the walk the horse moves his entire body. His legs move forward, by diagonals, one at a time. His spinal column moves from side to side like a snake in motion. His head and neck rock up and down and side to side for leverage, just as we human beings move our arms when walking.

Seat: To move in unison with the horse and to set the rhythm for the gait.

Legs: To maintain the forward motion.

Hands: To allow the horse's head movements while maintaining contact.

### When does the rider use the natural aids?

When the side-to-side rocking of the horse's hindquarters causes your weight to shift from one seat bone to the other, you must emphasize this motion with a stronger, but not faster, forward push with that seat bone. Your leg pressure on the corresponding side automatically increases when your seat bone moves forward. (Actually, you cannot move your seat bone forward without tightening the corresponding leg.) At the walk, the descending movement of the horse's head alternates to the left and right and you should follow these head movements with your hands, moving them discreetly forwards and backwards, left and right, "drawing," so to speak, the pattern of a sideways figure 8 (see Fig. 33).

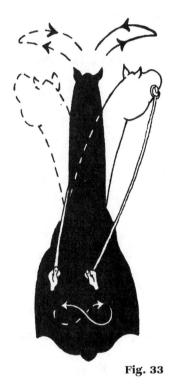

Fig. 33

## Using the Natural Aids at the Sitting Trot

### How does the rider use the natural aids?

Seat: Push the two seat bones forward every beat.

Legs: Continuously squeeze and release both calves simultaneously.

Hands: Keep your hands still at a fixed distance from the horse's mouth.

### Why does the rider use the natural aids?

At the trot the horse moves his legs by diagonal pairs. This gait has a springy action; the horse seems to be hopping from one diagonal to the other. The spinal column moves slightly up and down. The head has no particular action.

Seat: To sit comfortably without bouncing, and to give rhythm to the gait.

Legs: Squeeze the calves to keep the seat glued to the saddle, and to maintain the forward motion. Release to avoid fatigue and to keep the horse attentive.

Hands: At the trot, the horse does not need to rock his head for leverage, so the rider's hands remain still.

### When does the rider use the natural aids?

The springing action of the horse's trot causes the rider to bounce up and down. You must firmly push your seat bones forward every beat when you are about to leave the saddle. Leg pressure increases when your seat bones move forward and decreases when they move backwards.

## Using the Natural Aids at the Posting Trot

### How does the rider use the natural aids?

The posting trot is less tiring than the sitting trot for both horse and rider. You post by raising your seat out of the saddle every other beat (see Fig. 34).

Seat: Lean slightly forward, closing your hip angle. Lift yourself up and down with rhythm and smoothness.

**Fig. 34**

Legs: Release your legs when your seat is rising out of the saddle, increasing the weight on the stirrups; squeeze them together when your seat is coming down in contact with the saddle, lessening the weight on the stirrups.

Hands: Keep your hands still at a fixed distance from the horse's mouth.

### Why does the rider use the natural aids?

Seat: To avoid sitting one springing action out of two, which is less tiring for the rider and the horse's back.

Legs: Release together to lessen the effect of the springing action, and to keep the horse attentive; squeeze together to control the weight of the upper body, so as not to come down heavily on the horse's back, and to maintain the forward motion.

Hands: At the trot, the horse does not move his head.

### When does the rider use the natural aids?

A rider can post on either the right or the left diagonal pair of legs. *Tracking to the right, clockwise, you must post on the left diagonal. Tracking to the left, counterclockwise, you must post on the right diagonal.* Posting on the right diagonal, your seat and upper body rise when the horse's right diagonal moves forwards and come down into the saddle when the horse's right diagonal moves backwards. Posting on the left diagonal, your seat and upper body rise when the horse's left diagonal moves forward and come down into the saddle when the horse's left diagonal moves backwards.

Leg pressure increases when you come down into the saddle and decreases when you rise.

### How does the rider post on the correct diagonal?

To determine whether a diagonal is forward or back, glance at the point of your horse's shoulder. You can clearly see if the horse's shoulder is moving forwards or backwards (see Fig. 35). When you see the horse's left shoulder moving forwards, for example, the horse's left front foot is off the ground. When the left shoulder moves backwards, the horse's left front foot is on the ground.

 **Fig. 35**

You have two options if you find yourself posting on the wrong diagonal:

1. Sit down one extra beat, as is done by most riders.
2. Stay up out of the saddle one extra beat, preferable when riding a green horse and for sore riders.

When you become more experienced and relaxed, you will feel the motion of the two diagonals in your lower legs. You should be able to sense a very slight outward motion in your calves, created by the diagonal pair of legs on its way back. When you sense that slight outward motion with your left leg, for example, your horse's left shoulder is moving backwards. Rise immediately and you will be on the left diagonal.

### Why does the rider post on a specific diagonal?

When you post on the left diagonal, for example, this diagonal works a little harder than the right. When you are seated and the left diagonal is on the ground, the horse must exert more effort to lift this diagonal because of your weight. As soon as he has lifted the left diagonal, your weight is carried by the opposite diagonal, i.e. the right. The left diagonal becomes slightly off balance and moves more forward and to the left. As a result, this diagonal covers more ground and makes the horse bear slightly to the left. In a riding arena, one way to prevent your horse from coming toward the center would be to post on the outside diagonal.

If a rider, out of ignorance, carelessness, or comfort, always posted on the same diagonal, that pair of legs would develop more than the other. When asked to canter, the horse would have a definite tendency to take the same lead always and to travel sideways.

When trotting long distances, you should change diagonals from time to time so as not to tire one more than the other.

## Using the Natural Aids at the Canter

The rider has the option of cantering on either the right or left lead. As with the diagonal at the trot, the lead you choose depends on the direction your horse is traveling in. *Tracking to the right, clockwise, you should canter on the right lead. Tracking to the left, counterclockwise, you should canter on the left lead.*

The horse covers more ground with the leading lateral pair of legs. Knowing that the leading lateral is moving further forward than the other, you can easily determine what lead you are on by glancing at your horse's shoulders.

To remain straight at the canter, you can, if necessary, reposition your horse's nose and forehand to be in line with his hindquarters by using rein action ⓘⓘⓘ or ⓘᵥ .

To improve the rhythm of the canter, apply a series of light half-halts every few strides, using your outside rein (see page 41).

*Note: The instructions below are for the left lead canter. They should be reversed for the right lead.*

### How does the rider use the natural aids?

Seat: Push your seat bones forward every stride; the left is slightly more forward than the right.

Legs: Squeeze and release your legs together; the right leg should be slightly behind the girth.

Hands: Let your hands move forwards and backwards with the horse's head.

### Why does the rider use the natural aids?

Seat: By relaxing your lower back, maintaining the proper seat, and moving with your horse, you should clearly feel your seat bones rocking forward together. At the left lead canter, the horse has a tendency to travel slightly sideways, his haunches toward the left, creating a more pronounced rocking motion on your right seat bone than on the left. The seat, moving in unison with the horse's motion, sets the rhythm of the gait.

Legs: Act together to maintain the impulsion. The right leg stays a little further back than usual in order to compel the horse to keep the lead.

Hands: At the canter, like at the walk, the horse moves his head up and down for leverage and balance. Your hands, at a fixed distance from your horse's mouth, must yield to allow this motion while still maintaining contact.

### When does the rider use the natural aids?

At the canter, the horse's rocking motion causes the rider's seat to leave the saddle slightly. When you feel your seat leaving the saddle, you must push it forward, increasing your leg pressure. Your hands yield by moving forward when your horse's head moves down and returning to their original position when his head comes back up.

These seat, leg, and hand actions are simultaneous.

# The Natural Aids
# for Transitions

**A** **transition** is a change from one gait to the other, either upward or downward. Below are all the possible transitions, listed from the easiest to the most difficult:

| Upward Transitions | Downward Transitions |
|---|---|
| • Halt to walk. | • Walk to halt. |
| • Walk to trot. | • Trot to walk. |
| • Trot to canter. | • Canter to trot. |
| • Halt to trot. | • Canter to walk. |
| • Walk to canter. | • Trot to halt. |
| • Halt to canter. | • Canter to halt. |

## Upward Transitions

From a halt to a walk, a walk to a trot, and a halt to a trot, the aids are identical except for the amount of leg pressure applied.

Before an upward transition, you should get your horse to lower his neck slightly. By applying a light inside indirect rein ⑪ and an inside leg at the girth, you will put your horse on the bit and make him round his neck and spinal column.

Seat:  Stays relaxed and ready to follow the motion of the new gait.

Legs:  Act together at the girth until the desired gait is obtained.

Hands:   At first, yield to allow the forward motion and then act or resist to regulate it. *When changing from a sitting trot to a posting trot, you must shorten the reins to maintain the same contact.*

## Canter Departs

The upward transitions involving canter departs require more precision, because the horse can canter on either the left or right lead. The level of education of the horse and rider determines which aids are used: outside lateral aids, inside diagonal aids, or inside lateral aids.

*Note: All instructions below are for the left lead canter. They should be reversed for the right lead. The illustrations were designed for quick reference: the black foot indicates that that leg is performing functions other than simply maintaining the impulsion; the black dot on the saddle stands for the seat bone receiving more weight; and the black dot in front of the saddle indicates the active hand.*

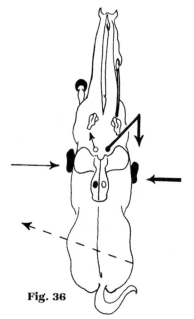

**Fig. 36**

### 1. Outside lateral aids (for young and green horses or beginner riders)

Seat:   More weight on the left seat bone.

Right leg:   Active behind the girth.

Left leg:   Active at the girth.

Right hand:   Active, applies a direct rein of opposition ⓘ.

Left hand:   Passive.

### How does the rider ask for a canter?

At the canter, the horse's leading lateral pair of legs reaches further forward than the other. To train a green horse successfully, you should place him in such a position that his balance is disturbed and he has to take the correct lead.

- Track counterclockwise so that your horse's left lateral pair of legs reaches further forward than the right.

- Pick up a posting trot on the right diagonal and set the proper rhythm.
- Before applying the outside lateral aids for the canter depart, switch to the left diagonal; you are now posting on the inside pair of legs, forcing the horse's left foreleg to reach even further forward. Your weight is on the left seat bone.
- Apply pressure behind the girth with your right leg to shift the horse's haunches slightly toward the left and to further engage his inside hind leg. Your left leg, active at the girth, pushes his inside foreleg forward.
- Apply a right direct rein of opposition ⓘ to impede the right shoulder (by burdening it) and give more freedom to the left one.
- Increase the pace of the trot to a maximum until the horse falls into the canter.

If your horse is "light" green (I mean semi-green—"dark" green, in my vocabulary, is a totally green horse), you can ask for the canter depart from a sitting trot.

## 2. Inside diagonal aids (for made horses and educated riders)

| | |
|---|---|
| Seat: | More weight on the right seat bone. |
| Right leg: | Active behind the girth. |
| Left leg: | Active at the girth. |
| Right hand: | Passive. |
| Left hand: | Active, applies an indirect rein of opposition in front of the withers ⓥ. |

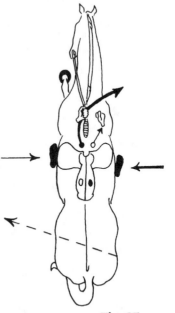

Fig. 37

## How does the rider ask for a canter?

- Track counterclockwise. You can pick up the canter from a sitting trot, walk, halt, rein back, or canter (for a flying change, see page 101).
- Stabilize the pace.
- Shift your weight to the right seat bone as well as to the right stirrup,

slowing the horse's outside lateral pair of legs and preventing an increase in speed.

- Slide your right leg behind the girth to displace the horse's haunches to the left and further engage his inside hind leg. Simultaneously, apply a left indirect rein of opposition in front of the withers ⓘⓥ to impede (by burdening it) the horse's right shoulder and give more freedom to the left one.
- Ask for the canter depart by acting with both legs.

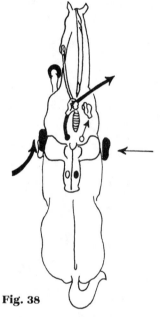

### 3. Inside lateral aids (for advanced horses and riders)

|  |  |
|---|---|
| Seat: | More weight on the right seat bone. |
| Right leg: | Active at the girth. |
| Left leg: | Active, slides forward toward the horse's left elbow. |
| Right hand: | Passive. |
| Left hand: | Active, applies an indirect rein of opposition in front of the withers ⓘⓥ. |

Using the inside lateral aids for the canter depart is my preferred method since, by sliding your inside leg forward, you have to lean back slightly, which helps stabilize the pace.

**Fig. 38**

### How does the rider ask for a canter?

- Track counterclockwise. You can pick up the canter from a sitting trot, walk, halt, rein back, or canter (for a flying change, see page 101).
- Stabilize the pace.
- Shift your weight to the right seat bone as well as to the right stirrup, slowing the horse's outside lateral pair of legs and preventing an increase in speed.
- Apply a left indirect rein of opposition in front of the withers ⓘⓥ to

impede (by burdening it) the horse's right shoulder and give more freedom to the left one.

- Ask for the canter depart by acting with both legs: your left leg slides forward toward the horse's left elbow, inciting him to pick up his leg, and your right leg applies pressure at the girth to maintain the impulsion.

---

*Imagine that a horse is standing on a cross-tie and a fly lands on his left elbow or on his left side where the girth would be if he were tacked. The horse is unable to bite at the fly because of the cross-tie and his tail is too short to reach it. He can shake his cutanius trunci muscle (the muscle below the skin), but the fly will simply return to the same spot a few seconds later. The best the horse can do is lift his left foreleg and kick it down to shake the fly off.*

*When a rider's leg slides forward and his or her foot touches the horse's elbow, the feeling on the horse's skin is similar. The reins prevent the horse from biting the rider's leg. The cutanius muscle and the tail have no effect. The horse can only pick up his left foreleg.*

---

When you reach a high level of riding, you can ask for a canter depart with equal leg pressure at the girth, followed immediately by a discreet hand signal (a quick rotation of the wrist, fingernails facing up) to determine the lead.

## Downward Transitions

From a walk to a halt, a trot to a walk, and a trot to a halt, the aids are identical except for the amount of leg pressure applied and the authority of the hands.

Seat: Weight is distributed equally on the two seat bones; lean back slightly.

Legs: Resist together at the girth to maintain engagement.

Hands: Act together to obtain the desired gait. *When changing from a posting trot to a sitting trot, you must lengthen the reins to maintain the same contact.*

When your horse comes to a halt, you should yield slightly with your hands and legs. If your horse has a tendency to halt crookedly, your hands correct his forehand and your legs correct the position of his hindquarters.

## Downward transitions from the canter

The downward transitions from the canter require more precision of the hands. From a canter to a trot, a canter to a walk, and a canter to a halt, the only difference in the action of the reins is in the distribution of the tension you apply.

*Note:   The instructions below are for downward transitions from the left lead canter. They should be reversed for the right lead.*

   Seat:   Sit deeper in the saddle, leaning back slightly.

   Legs:   Resist together at the girth to maintain engagement.

   Hands:   Act together, the left firmer than the right, to restrain the leading left lateral pair of legs.

*After all downward transitions, with the exception of those involving the halt, you should keep your horse attentive by maintaining a brisk pace at the slower gait for a few strides.*

# Part Three

# ADVANCED
# APPLICATIONS

**Y**ou can develop your horse's strength and improve the suppleness and smoothness of his movements with the following longitudinal and lateral exercises. The longitudinal exercises improve the flexibility of the spinal column and perfect the engagement. The lateral exercises improve the flexibility of the forehand and the hind legs and also perfect the engagement.

| Longitudinal Exercises | Lateral Exercises |
|---|---|
| • Lengthening and shortening. | • Shoulder-in. |
| • The rein back. | • Haunches-in. |
| | • Half-pass. |
| | • Half-turns (on the forehand and on the haunches). |

Instructions are also given for the counter-canter and the flying change of lead.

During the training period, keep in mind that you have to overcome the stiffness of your horse's muscular system as well as his occasional unwillingness. Whatever the horse needs to learn, it is wisest to divide the work over a period of a few days. Patience and perseverance are the keys to success.

*Note: The figures illustrating the rider's aids were designed for quick reference: the black foot indicates that that leg is performing functions other than simply maintaining the impulsion; and the black dot on the saddle stands for the seat bone receiving more weight.*

# The Natural Aids for Lengthening and Shortening

$\mathbf{A}$ horse is said to lengthen or shorten at the walk, trot, or canter when he shows variations in the size of his strides.

### Goals of the Exercise

- To develop the flexibility of the horse's spinal column.
- To develop the strength of the horse's hind legs (by lengthening).
- To develop the engagement (by shortening).
- To develop impulsion.
- To perfect the coordination of the rider's aids.

### How Does the Rider Lengthen and Shorten the Horse's Strides?

When you are tracking in a straight line, your leg and hand actions should never be simultaneous. In other words, when your legs act, your hands can resist but do not act, and when your hands act, your legs can resist but do not act. In a riding arena, you could divide the work as follows (see Fig. 39):

- On the long side of the arena, lengthen the strides by acting with both legs at the girth simultaneously. The hands, passive, may resist to prevent your horse from rushing.
- On the short side of the arena, shorten the strides by acting with

## Lengthening and Shortening

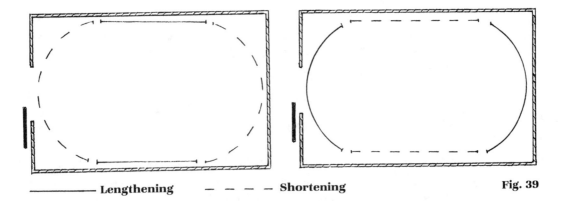

———————— Lengthening    — — — — Shortening

Fig. 39

both hands simultaneously to hold the pace. The legs stay in light contact to maintain the engagement.

- When you have repeated this exercise several times, your horse may anticipate your demands and respond faster. You can then reverse the order, asking for the shortening of the strides on the long side of the arena and the lengthening of the strides on the short side.

While you are practicing either lengthening or shortening:

- Keep your horse on the bit.
- Keep your horse straight (lateral pairs of legs parallel).
- Balance your horse between your legs and hands to regulate the gait and establish a rhythm.

These variations of stride can be executed at the walk, trot, or canter. When the horse is lengthening, you must allow some extension of the neck, without letting the horse put too much weight on his forehand. When the horse is shortening, you should allow his neck to rise slightly.

Fig. 40

At the beginning, your horse may react slowly to your commands. As the training progresses, the size of stride required should become easier to obtain. A prompt, yet smooth, response from the horse is a must. Abrupt changes should be avoided.

## Helpful Suggestions

When he lengthens, your horse must keep calm while at the same time reaching further forward with his legs than he normally does. If you let him rush, he will only multiply the number of steps he makes, which defeats the purpose of this exercise.

A lazy horse must work more on lengthening and a high-strung horse should work more on shortening.

If your horse has difficulty stretching one diagonal or lateral pair of legs, you should practice the lengthening on a circle tracking against the weak pair, e.g. for a weak left diagonal, you should work on a circle tracking to the right. You can also remedy this problem by cantering your horse on the lead opposite to the weak pair.

At the posting trot, to lengthen the stride more effectively and prevent too rapid a pace, you should sit longer in the saddle, so as to be slightly behind the horse's motion. This will make the horse work harder and stretch further without increasing his pace too much.

If you apply a left indirect rein ⓜ, you will increase the weight on the horse's right shoulder and allow the left one to move more freely. Apply a right indirect rein ⓜ to free the right shoulder. You can alternate these indirect reins to improve the lengthening or to begin the extended trot (a trot with maximum amplitude of stride and slow pace).

# The Natural Aids
# for the Rein Back

The rein back is a 2-phase movement in which the horse travels backwards by diagonal pairs of legs.

## Goals of the Exercise

- To develop the suppleness of the horse's spinal column.
- To improve the engagement of the horse's hind legs.
- To perfect the horse's balance.
- To improve the forward motion.

## Rider's Aids

Right hand: Resists. (Never pull!)

Left hand: Resists. (Never pull!)

Right leg: Active at the girth.

Left leg: Active at the girth.

Seat: Very light, achieved by increasing the weight in your heels.

## Why Does the Rider Use the Natural Aids?

Hands: To forbid any kind of forward motion.

Legs: To create the backward motion and to maintain the impulsion.

Seat: To lighten the rider's weight on the horse's back and to give freedom to his hind legs.

## How Does the Rider Initiate the Rein Back?

- The horse is at a halt, his hind legs engaged.
- The rider's legs act simultaneously to create impulsion.
- The hands resist simultaneously to prevent the horse from moving forward.
- The legs yield simultaneously to allow the backward motion of the horse.

Once the rein back is started, the motion is maintained by consistent, but intermittent, action of the legs. Alternating the action of the hands improves the lengthening of the stride. The right hand acts when the horse's right shoulder is forward, the left hand when the left shoulder is forward. *When the hands act, the legs resist, and vice versa.*

---

*Some people say, "To back a horse, the rider should not use any leg pressure." The legs create impulsion. If the horse does not need any impulsion to back, then these people are right. But let me ask you: Can you drive a car without stepping on the gas pedal?*

---

## How Does the Rider Teach the Rein Back?

This exercise is best taught from the ground first of all and should be practiced until the horse obeys without any hesitation.

- Standing left shoulder to left shoulder with the horse (facing the horse), hold both reins in your left hand, about 10 inches behind the horse's mouth, and carry a whip in your right hand.
- Apply tension on the reins toward the horse's rump and at the same time tap on his chest or belly with your whip.
- When the horse steps back a little, you should stop and reward him with a little pat on the neck. If the horse does not react, increase the

tension on the bit and tap more firmly on his chest or belly. If he is still reluctant, tap him on the legs below the knees or step on his hooves.

- When the horse is responding quickly, repeat the exercise holding the reins together above the withers. As soon as he feels the slightest tension on the bit, the horse should now step back.

    Practice the same exercise mounted.

- If the horse does not want to back because of your weight, move his haunches left and right with leg actions behind the girth. As soon as he moves his haunches, ask him to back.
- During the training period, your horse should back every day in short sessions consisting of two to four strides.

## Mistakes to Avoid

*The horse backs sideways.* If the horse does not back in a straight line, you should correct the direction of the backward motion by applying either an indirect rein ⓘ (neck rein) or an indirect rein of opposition in front of the withers ⓘⓥ to bring the shoulders in line with the haunches. You can also correct improper backing by sending the horse forward and applying a disciplinary leg action behind the girth on the same side toward which the horse has drifted.

*The rider pulls on the reins.* Under *no* circumstances should you pull on the

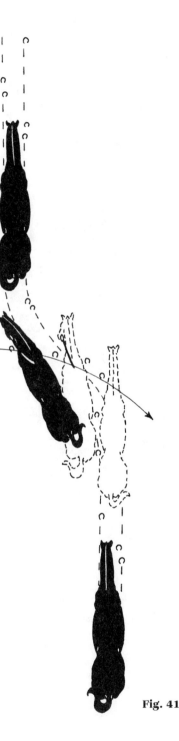

Fig. 41

**71**

reins to obtain a backing motion. An honest response to the rider's legs should produce satisfactory results. Pulling on the horse's mouth will only create resistance, making him hollow his back (an inadequate position for any kind of motion), and might cause him to rear.

Wrong                    Right

**Fig. 42**

## Helpful Suggestions

If a horse is unable or unwilling to move backward, it may simply be due to stiffness or lack of obedience to the rider's legs. Teaching him to move his haunches from one side to the other by practicing the half-turn on the forehand will remedy the matter (see page 93).

While backing, the horse must stay on the bit and be ready to move forward as soon as your hands yield.

You can start the rein back on any diagonal you choose. The action of the left direct rein of opposition ① and the right leg at the girth (diagonal aids) encourages the horse to begin the backward motion with his left diagonal pair of legs. Reverse the rein and leg for the right diagonal.

# The Natural Aids for the Shoulder-In

**A** horse is said to be in the shoulder-in when, going forward at the walk, trot, or canter, his forehand is toward the inside of the riding arena, and his entire spine is bent. The forelegs appear to be crossing each other, and the horse looks back in the direction he has come from.

## Goals of the Exercise

- To develop the suppleness of the horse's entire spinal column, permitting coordination between the forelegs and the hindquarters.
- To loosen and tone the horse's shoulder muscles.
- To further engage the horse's hind legs (especially the outside one).
- To improve inside lateral flexions.

*Note: The instructions below are for the lateral aids for a right shoulder-in. They should be reversed for a left shoulder-in.*

## Rider's Aids

| | |
|---|---|
| Right hand: | Active, applies an indirect rein of opposition behind the withers ⊙. |
| Left hand: | Passive, goes forward and down. |
| Right leg: | Active at the girth. |
| Left leg: | Active slightly behind the girth. |
| Seat: | More weight on the left seat bone. |

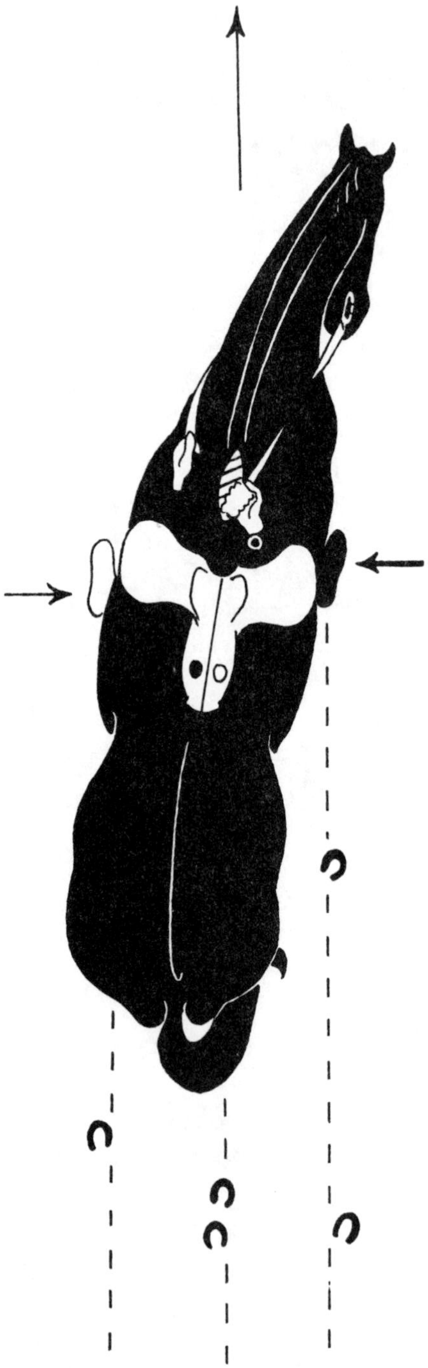

Fig. 43

## Why Does the Rider Use the Natural Aids?

Right hand: To maintain the bending of the neck to the right, and still keep the horse on the track.

Left hand: To allow and then to regulate the action of the right hand.

Right leg: To encourage bending and to maintain the impulsion.

Left leg: To prevent the haunches from drifting to the left and to maintain the impulsion.

Seat: To change the horse's balance and make him maintain the original direction.

## How Does the Rider Initiate the Shoulder-In?

- Establish the pace.
- Apply a right direct rein ⊙ to bend the horse to the right, legs active at the girth.
- In order to stay on the original track, resist with both hands as soon as the horse begins turning to the right and change the right direct rein ⊙ to a right indirect rein of opposition behind the withers ⊙.
- Maintain the action of the right hand and apply the aids as described on page 73.

## How Does the Rider Teach the Shoulder-In?

To avoid a common problem, that of the horse leaving the track, you should start training using an artificial aid, such as a wall

## The Shoulder-In

or the fence enclosing the riding arena, and ask the horse for a shoulder-out or counter shoulder-in (i.e. with his forehand toward the outside of the track).

- At the walk, tracking counterclockwise, have the horse travel straight, approximately 4 feet inside the normal track (see Fig. 44).

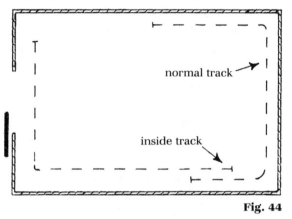

Fig. 44

- Begin the exercise by applying a right direct rein ⊙ to bring the horse's forehand to the right (toward the fence).
- When the horse's forehand has turned to the right, change the right direct rein ⊙ to a right indirect rein of opposition behind the withers ⊙ and simultaneously apply the aids of the right shoulder-in (see page 73). The horse will be traveling sideways with his spine bent to the right at an angle of 25 to 35 degrees from the wall. The right foreleg is on the normal track (see Fig. 45) and the left foreleg and hind legs are on the inside track. (A horse can travel on either 3 or 4 tracks, i.e., each foot can be in a different path.)

Fig. 45

75

▪ To avoid muscular contractions and resistance, have the horse travel only a few steps in this position. Then straighten the horse by a right indirect rein ⓜ (always bringing the shoulders in line with the haunches) and go forward at the trot. A little pat on the neck in reward would be most appropriate.

Practice the same exercise over a period of days and every day gradually increase the number of steps. As soon as the horse shows good results along the wall or fence, it is time to practice the same exercise farther and farther away from it. If necessary, the left hand, passive, can resist to control the bending of the neck and the direction of the motion. Once the horse has learned the shoulder-out, reverse the direction (track clockwise) and ask for a right shoulder-in.

This exercise must be practiced in both directions at the walk, trot, and canter. The stiff side of the horse should be worked more than the other for better symmetrical development.

To reinforce the lesson, teach the horse to switch from a shoulder-in to a shoulder-out and vice versa. You can also ask for transitions, maintaining the shoulder-in or shoulder-out before, during, and after the command.

## Mistakes to Avoid

**Fig. 46**

Wrong

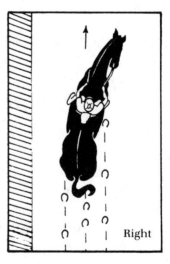
Right

***The horse travels straight with his neck bent.*** When the horse is in a shoulder-in, his entire spinal column must be bent, i.e. from the head to the tail. You must make sure that your horse is not bending only his neck. If this is the case, the action will stop at the withers and will affect neither the shoulders nor the engagement. Switching the passive rein to an indirect rein ⓜ will remedy the matter.

***The rider's weight is on the wrong seat bone.*** You must make sure that your weight is on the proper seat bone. For the right shoulder-in, it should be on the left seat bone; for the left shoulder-in, it should be on the right seat bone.

---

*For the exercises in this book I have described work on the horse's right side to make it easier for the reader to refer to the instructions for the five different rein actions. However, it is generally easier to start any kind of exercise with the horse's left side because, except in some rare cases, horses are more supple on the left side than on the right. The reason for this could be that foals are curled to the left in their mother's womb.*

---

## Helpful Suggestions

The horse should wear galloping boots during the training session to protect his legs against clumsiness. If he bangs his legs, he may get frightened and rush.

At a shoulder-in, a trained horse should travel sideways on 3 tracks at an angle of 30 to 35 degrees. Traveling on 4 tracks is only a matter of showmanship.

To attain all the goals of this exercise, the horse must have strong impulsion and the pace must be accelerated.

When your horse shies or drifts away from a specific point, you can "block" him by applying the aids for a shoulder-in.

# The Natural Aids for the Haunches-In

**A** horse is said to be in the haunches-in when, going forward at the walk, trot, or canter, his haunches are towards the inside of the riding arena and his spinal column is straight. His hind legs appear to be crossing each other and the horse looks straight ahead. The haunches-in is also called *travers*. Executed on an inside track, haunches facing out, it is called a haunches-out or *renvers*.

## Goals of the Exercise

- To put more emphasis on the action of the horse's hind legs (especially the inside one) and to improve the engagement.
- To improve flexions.
- To overcome clumsiness caused by the rider's weight.
- To prepare for the half-pass.
- To teach obedience to the action of the rider's legs behind the girth.
- To teach the rider precise use of the aids.

*Note: The instructions below are for the diagonal aids for a right haunches-in. They should be reversed for a left haunches-in.*

## Rider's Aids

Right hand:   Active, applies a light indirect rein ⑪.
Left hand:   Passive, goes forward and down.

## The Haunches-In

Right leg:   Active at the girth.

Left leg:   Active behind the girth.

Seat:   More weight on the right seat bone.

## Why Does the Rider Use the Natural Aids?

Right hand:   To bring the horse's nose and head to the right and to maintain the forehand on the original track.

Left hand:   To allow and then to regulate the action of the right hand.

Right leg:   To create and maintain the impulsion.

Left leg:   To move the haunches to the right, and to maintain an inside track.

Seat:   To encourage the horse to maintain the original direction.

## How Does the Rider Initiate the Haunches-In?

- Track to the right and establish a pace.
- Slide your left leg behind the girth to displace the haunches slightly to the right.
- Apply the aids as described above.

## How Does the Rider Teach the Haunches-In?

The horse has first to learn to move his haunches in response to any action of the

**Fig. 47**

**Fig. 48**

leg behind the girth. Begin this initial exercise from the ground.

- Standing left shoulder to left shoulder with the horse, hold the left rein in your left hand and carry a whip in your right hand.
- Walking backwards, ask the horse to follow you by applying tension on the left rein (the horse moves forward when you move backwards).
- Touch the horse's left hind leg with the whip to encourage him to move his haunches to the right. When the horse does so, you should stop and reward him with a little pat on the neck.

This exercise should be practiced several times until the horse is no longer frightened by the action of the whip and moves his haunches to the side at your command.

You should then practice the same exercise mounted.

- Act with your left leg behind the girth to make the horse move his haunches to the right.
- With practice, your horse should yield to your leg the way he yielded to the whip.

This exercise must be taught on the right side as well. When the horse yields properly to the action of the leg behind the girth, it is time to start teaching the haunches-in.

- Tracking clockwise in a riding arena, slow the horse to facilitate the execution of the movement.
- Simultaneously apply a right indirect

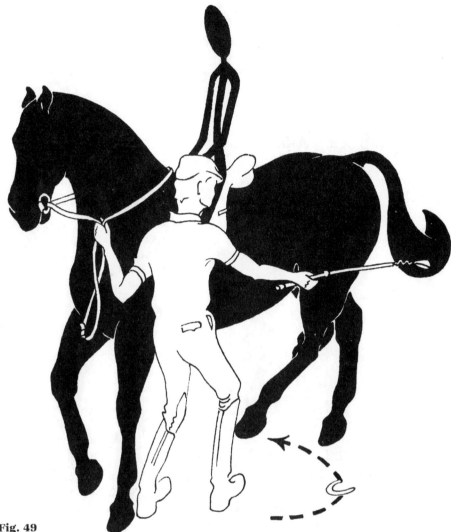

**Fig. 49**

rein ⑪ and act with your left leg behind the girth to make the horse swing his haunches to the right. The horse should travel sideways at an angle of 30 to 35 degrees from the wall. His forehand is on the normal track, and his haunches on the inside track.

- To avoid muscular contractions and resistance, have the horse travel only a few steps in this position. Then straighten him with a left indirect rein ⑪ to bring his shoulders in line with his haunches, bring your left leg forward so it is at the girth, and send your horse forward at a trot. A little pat on the neck in reward would be appropriate.

Practice the same exercise over a period of days, gradually adding to the number of steps.

## Mistakes to Avoid

***The horse looks in the wrong direction.*** You must make sure that your horse's head is on the proper side. For the right haunches-in, his head should be to the right; for the left haunches-in, his head should be to the left.

**Fig. 50**

***The rider's weight is on the wrong seat bone.*** Make sure that your weight is on the proper seat bone. For the right haunches-in, your weight should be on the right seat bone; for the left haunches-in, your weight should be on the left seat bone.

## Helpful Suggestions

The horse should wear galloping boots during the training session to protect his legs against clumsiness. If he bangs his legs he may get frightened and rush.

## The Haunches-In

At a haunches-in or haunches-out, a trained horse should travel on 3 tracks at an angle of 30 to 35 degrees. Traveling on 4 tracks is only a matter of showmanship.

An educated rider should practice leg yielding (see page 15) as the sole aid to initiate the haunches-in or haunches-out.

To attain all the goals of this exercise, the horse must have strong impulsion and the pace must be accelerated.

# The Natural Aids for the Half-Pass

**A** horse is said to be in a half-pass when he is going forward obliquely at the walk, trot, or canter. His shoulders and haunches make two parallel tracks, and his spinal column is straight. His forelegs as well as his hind legs appear to be crossing each other. The horse looks in the direction he is traveling.

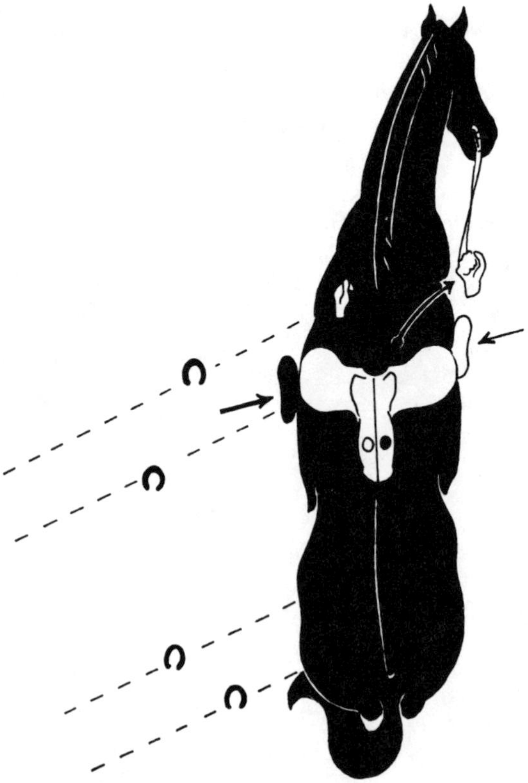

Fig. 51

### Goals of the Exercise

- To reinforce the horse's training in the lateral movements (on two tracks).
- To improve the suppleness of the horse's spinal column.
- To teach the rider precise use of the aids.

*Note: The instructions below are for a half-pass to the right. They should be reversed for a half-pass to the left.*

### Rider's Aids

Right hand: Active, applies a direct rein (I).

Left hand: Passive, goes forward and down. If necessary, switches to an indirect rein (III).

Right leg: Active at the girth.

Left leg: Active behind the girth.

Seat: More weight on the right seat bone.

## Why Does the Rider Use the Natural Aids?

Right hand: To lead the horse and to bring his nose and head to the right (right bend).

Left hand: To allow the forehand to go forward and to the right; to regulate the action of the right hand. If needed, the left hand will act alternately with the right hand with an indirect rein ⓜ to push the horse's shoulder to the right.

Right leg: To create and maintain the impulsion.

Left leg: To make the horse move his haunches to the right.

Seat: To encourage the horse to bear to the right.

## How Does the Rider Initiate the Half-Pass?

- Tracking clockwise, have the horse travel straight (lateral pairs of legs parallel). (See Fig. 52.)
- Establish the pace.
- At the end of the short side of the arena, ask for a right shoulder-in.
- Pass the corner in this position.
- At the beginning of the long side of the arena, apply a right direct rein ⊙ and leave the track to follow a diagonal line across the arena (see Fig. 53). When the horse's forehand leaves the track, slide your left leg behind the girth.
- Going diagonally across the arena, maintain the aids for the half-pass to the right (see Fig. 54).

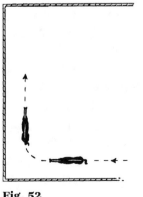

Fig. 52

Fig. 53

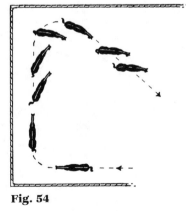

Fig. 54

Fig. 55

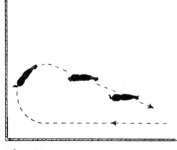

Fig. 56

*Trainers' opinions are divided on when to begin working on the half-pass. For the shoulder-in, the horse works mainly with his forelegs. For the haunches-in, the horse works mainly with his hind legs. For the half-pass, the horse combines the two. In my opinion, the half-pass is the synthesis of all the lateral work. Therefore, it should be taught after the horse has learned the shoulder-in and the haunches-in.*

## How Does the Rider Teach the Half-Pass?

- Teach and perfect the shoulder-in and shoulder-out.
- Teach and perfect the haunches-in and haunches-out.
- Teach and perfect the switch from a shoulder-in to a shoulder-out.
- Teach and perfect the switch from a haunches-in to a haunches-out.
- Teach and perfect the switch from a shoulder-in to a haunches-in.
- Teach and perfect the switch from a shoulder-out to a haunches-out.
- Teach and perfect the switch from a shoulder-in to a haunches-out.
- Teach and perfect the switch from a shoulder-out to a haunches-in.
- Tracking clockwise, ask the horse to reverse by making a right half-turn of about 30 feet and begin a right shoulder-in. On the oblique line going back to the track, make your horse execute a few steps of half-pass to the right by applying a right direct rein ⊙, and then your left leg behind the girth. (See Fig. 56.)

▪ Ask for a half-pass on the diagonal line across the arena (see page 85).

When you first begin training, the fence around the arena is an excellent aid, but too much dependence on it may make your horse lazy. As soon as possible, you must work your horse away from the fence. Use of the passive rein, which regulates both direction and impulsion, is mandatory for lateral work. In the case of the half-pass, the passive rein may have to be switched to an indirect rein ⑩ to keep the horse's shoulders slightly ahead of his haunches. This action should alternate with the active rein.

## Mistakes to Avoid

*The horse has poor head carriage.*   Make sure your horse is on the bit.

*The horse looks in the wrong direction.*   You must make sure your horse's head is on the proper side. For a half-pass to the right, his head should be to the right; for a half-pass to the left, his head should be to the left.

*The horse's haunches lead his shoulders.*   To solve this problem, you should alternate a few steps of half-pass with a few steps on a straight track.

Wrong

Right

**Fig. 57**

***The rider's weight is on the wrong seat bone.*** You must make sure that your weight is on the proper seat bone. For the half-pass to the right, your weight is on the right seat bone; for the half-pass to the left, your weight is on the left seat bone.

## Helpful Suggestions

The horse should wear galloping boots during the training sessions to protect his legs against clumsiness. If he bangs his legs, he may get frightened and rush.

Both the horse and the rider should look straight ahead. The horse must have strong impulsion and the pace must be accelerated in order to attain all the goals of this exercise.

The horse's forehand must always slightly precede his haunches. If his shoulders lead too much, he is *not yet* in a half-pass. If his haunches lead, he is *no longer* in a half-pass.

When you ask for the half-pass, you should make sure that the leg behind the girth begins to act *after* your hands. Otherwise, the horse's haunches could precede his shoulders.

At the half-pass, a trained horse should be at an angle of 30 to 40 degrees from the original track.

# The Natural Aids for the Half-Turn on the Haunches

This exercise is not a prerequisite for brilliant lateral work but is mentioned for reference and for those who wish to achieve greater precision in the leg action behind the girth.

The half-turn on the haunches consists of a very short turn from a halt. The forehand of the horse rotates 180 degrees around the haunches. When this exercise is executed at a walk or a canter it is known as the half-pirouette.

In a turn from the left track to the right track, the horse is said to pivot on his left hind foot (from the right track to the left track, he pivots on his right hind foot). In reality, the horse moves all 4 feet up and down. When the horse executes this exercise from the halt, the pivotal foot, while moving up and down, comes back down on the same spot. At any other gait, the horse's pivotal foot moves less than his other feet in any direction.

## Goals of the Exercise

- To increase the mobility and lightness of the forehand.
- To improve flexions.

*Note: The instructions below are for a half-turn on the haunches toward the inside of the riding arena, from the left track to the right track. They should be reversed for a half-turn from the right track to the left track.*

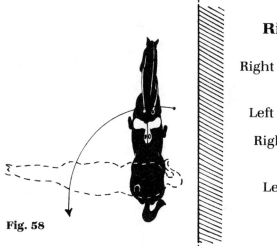

Fig. 58

## Rider's Aids

Right hand: Active, applies an indirect rein ⃝.

Left hand: Resists lightly.

Right leg: Active slightly behind the girth.

Left leg: Active at the girth.

Seat: More weight on the left seat bone.

## Why Does the Rider Use the Natural Aids?

Right hand: To make the horse's shoulder go to the left.

Left hand: To regulate the action of the right hand and to maintain a slight bending to the left.

Right leg: To prevent the haunches from drifting to the right.

Left leg: To create and maintain the impulsion.

Seat: To encourage the horse to go to the left.

## How Does the Rider Initiate a Half-Turn on the Haunches?

- Tracking counterclockwise (unless you are at a halt), first ask for a few steps of shoulder-in.
- Simultaneously apply a right indirect rein ⃝ and a right leg behind the girth.
- Put the horse into the half-turn, making sure that you maintain the impulsion and the direction of the motion. Remember to keep the horse's nose on the left.

## How Does the Rider Teach the Half-Turn on the Haunches?

- Teach and perfect the action of the indirect rein ⑩. To do this, practice "zigzagging," alternately using the left and the right indirect rein ⑩, first at the walk and then at the trot and canter.
- Practice the half-turn using only the indirect rein ⑩ and the corresponding leg behind the girth.
- As your horse understands better, reduce the diameter of the half-circle to the point that you can do it from a halt.
- From a halt, ask the horse to move and make only one step, then stop.
- Ask for another step and stop again, and so on.
- When the horse can quietly execute a half-turn, step by step, without trying to escape the aids, ask for the same exercise, two steps at a time, then three, and so on.

*The horse must learn to execute these half-turns equally well on both sides.*

## Mistakes to Avoid

***The horse steps backwards.*** You must not allow any backward motion during the progression of the half-turn on the haunches. If the horse has a tendency to step backwards, stop the exercise, send him forward, and start the half-turn all over again.

***The horse crosses his forelegs backwards or doesn't cross them at all (side-steps).*** Increasing the impulsion with your inside active leg at the girth will remedy the matter.

***The horse turns on the wrong pivotal foot.*** To correct this, increase both the pressure of the leg behind the girth and the weight on the opposite seat bone.

## Helpful Suggestions

The horse should wear galloping boots during the training sessions to protect his legs against clumsiness. If he bangs his legs, he may get frightened and rush.

You must always look for maximum crossing of the horse's legs so that he gets the greatest benefit possible from this exercise.

# The Natural Aids for the Half-Turn on the Forehand

This exercise is not a prerequisite for brilliant lateral work, but is mentioned for reference and for those who wish to achieve greater precision in the leg action behind the girth.

The half-turn on the forehand consists of a very short turn from the halt. The horse's haunches rotate 180 degrees around his forehand. When this exercise is executed at a walk it is known as the half-pirouette in reverse.

In a turn from the right track to the left track, the horse is said to pivot on his left forefoot (from the left track to the right track, he pivots on his right forefoot). In reality, the horse moves all four feet up and down. When the horse executes this exercise from a halt, the pivotal foot, while moving up and down, comes back down on the same spot. When the half-turn is executed at the walk, the horse's pivotal foot describes a smaller circle than any other foot.

## Goals of the Exercise

- To perfect the horse's obedience to the rider's legs.
- To increase the mobility of the horse's hindquarters.
- To improve engagement.
- To improve flexions.

   *Note:   The instructions below are for a half-turn toward the*

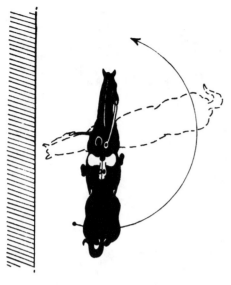

*inside from the right track to the left track. They should be reversed for a half-turn from the left track to the right track.*

## Rider's Aids

| | |
|---|---|
| Right hand: | Active, applies an indirect rein of opposition in front of the withers ⓘⓥ. |
| Left hand: | Passive, goes forward and down. |
| Right leg: | Active at the girth. |
| Left leg: | Active behind the girth. |
| Seat: | More weight on the right seat bone. |

**Fig. 59**

## Why Does the Rider Use the Natural Aids?

| | |
|---|---|
| Right hand: | To keep the weight on the horse's left front leg (the pivotal leg) and to keep the horse's nose slightly to the right. |
| Left hand: | To allow and then to regulate the action of the right hand, as well as to control the bending of the neck. |
| Right leg: | To create impulsion and to prevent the horse from stepping backwards. |
| Left leg: | To move the horse's haunches to the right and to make them turn around the forehand. |
| Seat: | To encourage the horse to go to the right. |

## How Does the Rider Initiate a Half-Turn on the Forehand?

The half-turn on the forehand should be demanded from an inside track so that the horse is not bothered by the fence of the arena.

- Tracking clockwise, apply the left leg behind the girth and the right indirect rein of opposition in front of the withers ⓘᵥ.
- Squeeze and release the left leg behind the girth until the half-turn is completed.

## How Does the Rider Teach the Half-Turn on the Forehand?

- Teach and perfect the horse's response to leg action behind the girth (see page 80 under **How Does the Rider Teach the Haunches-In?**).
- Practice the use of your diagonal aids by doing the haunches-in.
- Execute a series of half-turns in that position and progressively reduce the diameter of the circle until the horse is able to do it from a halt.
- From a halt, ask the horse to move and make only one step, then stop.
- Ask for another step and stop again, and so on.
- When the horse can quietly execute a half-turn, step by step, without trying to escape the aids, ask for the same exercise, two steps at a time, and so on.

*The horse must learn to execute these half-turns equally well on both sides.*

### Mistakes to Avoid

**The horse steps backward.**  You must not allow any backward motion during the progression of the half-turn on the forehand. If the horse has a tendency to step backward, stop the exercise, send him forward, and start the half-turn all over again.

**The horse crosses his hind legs backwards or doesn't cross them at all (side-steps).**  Acting firmly with your inside leg at the girth will increase the impulsion and remedy the matter.

**The horse turns on the wrong pivotal foot.**  Insisting on the inside indirect rein of opposition in front of the withers ⓘᵥ will over-burden the outside foreleg and force the horse onto the correct foot.

## Helpful Suggestions

The horse should wear galloping boots during the training session to protect his legs against clumsiness. If he bangs his legs, he may get frightened and rush.

You must always look for maximum amplitude in the crossing of the horse's legs so that he gets the greatest benefit possible from this exercise.

# The Natural Aids for the Counter-Canter

The horse is said to be at the counter-canter (or on the wrong lead) when he is cantering on the left lead, tracking clockwise, or on the right lead, tracking counterclockwise. The counter-canter is a very good exercise for developing and improving the rider's skills.

## Goals of the Exercise

- To improve the horse's balance.
- To make the horse supple in his entire length.
- To improve flexions.
- To teach the horse to canter straight and quietly.
- To prepare for the flying change of lead.

*Note: The instructions below are for a left lead canter, tracking clockwise. They should be reversed for a right lead canter, tracking counterclockwise.*

## Rider's Aids

The aids are the same as for any canter depart; however, the action of the leg behind the girth should be more emphasized and the horse's nose should stay on the same side as the lead on which he is cantering.

Right hand:   Passive.

Left hand:   Active, applies an indirect rein of opposition in front of the withers ⓥ.

Right leg:   Active behind the girth.

Left leg:   Active at the girth.

Seat:   More weight on the right seat bone.

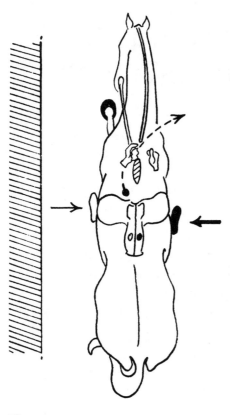

**Fig. 60**

## Why Does the Rider Use the Natural Aids?

Right hand:   To allow and to regulate the action of the left hand.

Left hand:   To overburden the horse's right shoulder and slow it down, and to free the left one.

Right leg:   To shift the horse's haunches to the left and signal the canter depart.

Left leg:   To create and maintain the impulsion.

Seat:   To lighten the weight on the horse's left lateral pair of legs and make it easier for the horse to balance himself.

## How Does the Rider Initiate the Counter-Canter?

- Tracking clockwise, place your horse in a haunches-out (*renvers*).
- Apply the left diagonal aids for the canter depart.

**98**

## How Does the Rider Teach the Counter-Canter?

First, perfect the horse's obedience to the indirect rein ⓜ. To do so, tracking counter-clockwise, trot on the long side of the arena and have your horse leave the track and make for the center, then turn and return to the track (see Fig. 61):

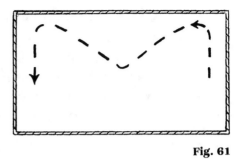

**Fig. 61**

- To leave the track, simultaneously apply a right indirect rein ⓜ, with your right leg more active at the girth than the left.
- To go back to the track, simultaneously apply a left indirect rein ⓜ, with your left leg more active at the girth than the right.

Do the same work at the canter in both directions, using slightly different aids:

- To leave the track, simultaneously apply a right indirect rein ⓜ, with your right leg more active behind the girth than the left.
- To go back to the track, simultaneously apply a left indirect rein ⓜ with your *right* leg more active behind the girth than the left.

Make sure that the horse does not break the gait or change lead. As the horse progresses in this exercise, you should become more demanding and decrease the angle of the turn in the center of the arena (see Fig. 62).

When the changes of direction in the middle of the arena become easy and automatic, it is time to ask for the counter-canter.

- Cantering counterclockwise, reverse the direction *without changing lead* by making

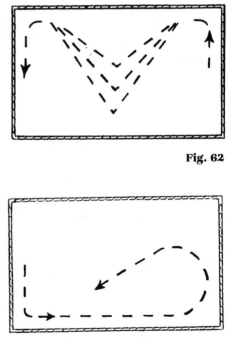

**Fig. 62**

**Fig. 63**

a half-circle to your left at the end of the long side of the arena (see Fig. 63).

- To maintain the original lead, keep a slow pace and concentrate on maintaining the pressure of the right leg behind the girth, which was applied to signal the canter depart.
- Keep the horse's nose on the same side as the lead on which he is cantering.

After the horse has reversed direction and returned to the original track, he may cut the corner to pass the short side of the arena. You should let him. With time and practice, you should be able to stay on the track. Once you can, move on to the following exercise.

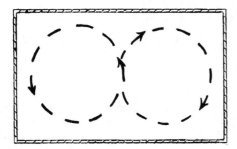

**Fig. 64**

- Counter-canter on a figure 8 across the arena, starting on the correct lead (see Fig. 64).
- Progressively reduce the size of the figure 8, until you feel satisfied with your horse's performance.

This series of exercises should be executed over a period of a few days to prevent the horse from developing muscular contractions.

## Mistakes to Avoid

***The horse does not maintain the lead or breaks the gait.*** First you should make sure that *you* are not responsible. Repeat the exercise and insist with a very strong active leg behind the girth, making sure not to interfere with any unnecessary hand action.

## Helpful Suggestions

If your horse has difficulty performing the counter-canter on one lead or the other, practicing the shoulder-in to the opposite side for a few days will easily remedy the matter.

# The Natural Aids for the Flying Change of Lead

**A** flying change of lead is a canter depart executed when the horse is already at the canter. The horse changes from one lead to the other without breaking the gait.

## Goals of the Exercise

- To improve the horse's balance when changing direction.
- To prepare the horse for the High School Dressage.

*Note: The instructions below are for a flying change from the left lead to the right. They should be reversed for a flying change from the right lead to the left.*

## Rider's Aids

The aids described below are applied when the horse is already cantering. The best time for the horse to change leads is during the fourth phase of the canter, when all 4 feet are off the ground. You should ask for the flying change of lead a little before the suspension phase, i.e. during the third phase, when only one of the horse's forefeet is on the ground. To be successful, you must be able to feel clearly the 4 phases of the canter, and you must have good reflexes. Rapid and precise application of the natural aids is mandatory to obtain a flying change.

| | |
|---|---|
| Right hand: | Becomes active, applies an indirect rein of opposition in front of the withers ⓘⱽ. |
| Left hand: | Becomes passive, controls the forward motion. |
| Right leg: | Becomes active at the girth. |
| Left leg: | Active and stronger, moves behind the girth. |
| Seat: | Becomes lighter, achieved by increasing the weight in the stirrups. |

## How Does the Rider Initiate the Flying Change of Lead?

- Put your horse into a left lead canter.
- Slightly reduce the pace.
- If necessary, execute a firm half-halt to perfect the horse's balance or to bring extra weight from his forehand to his hind legs. Follow immediately with a slight increase in the pace.
- When the horse is about to enter the suspension phase, apply the aids for a right lead canter as described above.

## How Does the Rider Teach the Flying Change of Lead?

- Teach and perfect the canter depart on both leads from a trot, a walk, a halt, and a rein back.
- Teach and perfect the counter-canter on both leads.

When the horse can execute the counter-canter correctly on both leads, practice simple changes of lead.

- From a left lead canter, bring the horse back to a trot and keep this gait for a few steps. Then ask for either a left or a right lead canter.
- When this exercise becomes easy for the horse, be more demanding and ask for the transitions from a walk and then from a halt.
- As the horse improves at the simple changes, progressively reduce the number of steps of the trot and the walk between the changes.
- To break the monotony and to avoid having the horse anticipate your commands, vary the exercises. Instead of going from one lead to the

opposite one every time, ask for the same lead several times in a row: left lead, trot or walk, right lead, trot or walk, and then right lead again; or left lead, trot or walk, left lead again, trot or walk, right lead, and so on.

When the horse is very comfortable with the simple changes of lead from the walk, you can ask for the first flying change.

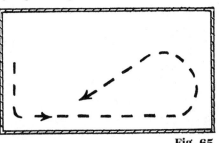

Fig. 65

- Start to canter on the lead the horse likes best.
- At the end of the long side of the riding arena, reverse the direction by making a half-turn of about 30 feet (see Fig. 65).
- When the horse comes back to the track, ask for a change of lead without breaking the gait.
- After cantering a few strides on the new lead, return to a walk and reward generously.
- Repeat this exercise in both directions until the horse becomes familiar with it.

To perfect the flying change of lead, practice the following set of exercises in the order given, going from the simplest to the most difficult.

- Ask for a flying change on a circle from a counter-canter.
- Ask for a flying change on a straight line from a counter-canter.
- Ask for a flying change on a straight line from the correct lead.
- Ask for a flying change on a circle from the correct lead.
- Ask for flying changes from the wrong lead to the correct lead and back to the wrong lead.
- Ask for flying changes from the correct lead to the wrong lead and back to the correct lead.

## Mistakes to Avoid

***The horse changes lead with his forelegs first.*** A good flying change starts with the hind legs. An easy way to re-school a horse that has the tendency to switch the lead with his forelegs first is to ask for the changes of lead when the horse is at a counter-canter in a haunches-out.

***The horse rushes after changing the lead.*** Repeating the exercise frequently will solve the problem.

## Helpful Suggestions

For a good flying change, both horse and rider must stay calm.

Ask for a little at a time, be patient, and reward your horse generously. Repeat the exercise until satisfactory performance is obtained.

At the beginning, apply outside lateral aids (see page 58) to change lead. Later, you should switch to the diagonal aids (see page 59) or the inside lateral aids (see page 60).

Be firm with your legs.

When you have perfected the simple flying change of lead, you can ask for changes at close intervals. The flying change executed every stride belongs to the High School Dressage, along with the *piaffe* and the *passage*.

# Concluding Remarks

**B**efore closing this book, remember:

- A good seat gives the impression that the rider is part of the horse.
- A well-trained horse should respond to light leg pressure. Force is necessary only when your horse has been poorly trained.
- A good leg has proper timing.
- A good hand is a light hand. Suppose for a moment that the reins were made of a strand of thread and the end were held by someone you love. Would you break it?
- Your hands should always act intermittently.
- Your legs should always be more active than your hands.

# Index

# Index

# Index

# Index

## About the Author

François Lemaire de Ruffieu grew up in France. He was first trained by Maître Jean Couillaud and graduated in 1967 from the Cadre Noir, one of the oldest and most prestigious riding academies in Europe. During his six years in the cavalry at Saumur and Fontainebleau, he studied and showed extensively in dressage, stadium jumping, three-day eventing, and steeplechase. He also taught riding in Paris at the Military School of War. Since coming to the United States in 1971, he has broken and trained yearlings, ridden as a jockey at several racetracks, and taught at numerous stables. In 1978 he started his own business and now spends most of his time giving clinics throughout the United States and Europe. His students have won year-end high-score awards in equitation, hunter classes, stadium jumping, dressage, and combined training.